green guide

BIRDS

· ·

OF AUSTRALIA

Peter Rowland
Series Editor: Louise Egerton

NEW
HOLLAND

Barnes & Noble

Published in Australia in 1998 by
New Holland Publishers (Australia) Pty Ltd
Sydney • Auckland • London • Cape Town

14 Aquatic Drive Frenchs Forest NSW 2086 Australia
218 Lake Road Northcote Auckland New Zealand
24 Nutford Place London W1H 5DQ United Kingdom
80 McKenzie Street Cape Town 8001 South Africa

Reprinted in 1999 and 2000

National Library of Australia Cataloguing-in-Publication Data:

Rowland, Peter, 1967–.
Birds of Australia
Includes index
ISBN 1 86436 343 6

1. Birds—Australia 2. Birds—Australia—Identification
I. Title. (Series: Green guide).

598.0994

Project Manager: Fiona Doig
Series Editor: Louise Egerton
Design and Cartography: Tricia McCallum
Cover Design: Peta Nugent
Picture Researcher: Bronwyn Rennex
Reproduction: DNL Resources
Printed and bound by Times Offset (M) Sdn. Bhd.

Photographic Acknowledgments
Abbreviations: NHIL = New Holland Image Library, NF = Nature Focus, LT = Lochman Transparencies.
Photograph positions: t = top, b = bottom, m = main, i = inset, fc = front cover, bc = back cover

Shaen Adey/NHIL: p. 15i, 16, 24i, 36i, 70b; **Kathie Atkinson**: p. 40–41; **G.B. Baker/NF**: p. 14–15; **Bill Belson/LT**: p. 75t; **Hans & Judy Beste/LT**: front flap, p. 39b, 71t; **Eva Boogaard/LT**: p. 39t; **Norman Chaffer Estate/NF**: p. 83t; **Graeme Chapman**: p. 18t, 19b, 22b, 37t, 41i, 42t, 49b, 56, 63t, 65b, 71b, 72b, 81t, 85b, 86t, 91b; **R. Drummond**: contents, fc l, p. 4, 5, 11b, 17t, 25t&b, 28m&i, 29b, 30–31, 32, 34t, 36m, 37b, 42b, 48i, 51t, 55b, 64t, 66m&i, 69i, 70t, 73t&b, 74t, 76i, 81b, 82m&i, 83b, 85t, 87, 92t; **Wayne Lawler/Ecopix**: p. 19t; **T & P Gardner/NF**: p. 45b; **Jiri Lochman/LT**: p. 24m, 64b, 75b; **Peter Marsack/ LT**: p. 76m; **John McCann**: p. 35m; *compliments of* **Minolta**: p. 93b; **National Library of Australia**: p. 61b; **NHIL**: p. 93t; **S. Peckover/NF**: p. 61t; **Trevor W. Pescott/NF**: p. 67t; **Mike Prociv/Wetro Pics**: p. 80t; **Bronwyn Rennex**: p. 18b, 38b; **P. Roberts**: p. 7t, 23, 27t, 29t, 33t, 34b, 35i, 46t, 50b, 53t, 65t, 67b, 72t; **P. Rowland**: p. 6, 21t&b; **Dennis Sarson/LT**: p. 26b; **M.Seyfort**: p. 20t, 27b, 33b, 44t&b, 45t, 46b, 47t&b, 48m, 49t, 50t, 52t&b, 53b, 55t, 57b, 58m&i, 59t, 62m, 63b, 68–69, 77t, 80b, 88i, 91t; **Raoul Slater/LT**: p. 54t; **Katie Smith**: p. 38t, back flap; **Geoff Taylor/LT**: p. 26t; **Glen Threlfo**: fc c, p. 7b, 22t, 59b, 78–79, 88m, 90t; **Dave Watts**: fc t&b, p. 8–9, 9i, 10, 11t, 12t&b, 13, 17b, 20b, 31i, 43t&b, 51b, 54b, 57t, 60t&b, 62i, 74b, 77b, 79i, 84m&i, 86b, 89t, 90b, 92b, 95, bc b; **Martin R Willis/NF**: p.89b.

CONTENTS

An Introduction to Birds

This guide is an introduction to the major groups of Australian birds with an emphasis on those the amateur naturalist and nature-lover is most likely to see. Birdwatching is a wonderful hobby and can be enjoyed by anyone. Some people spend every minute they can spare at the beach or in a rainforest looking for birds in a desperate effort to see every species, while for others it is merely a casual interest. It is for this latter group that this book is intended, but be warned — that's how I started!

Bird Diversity

Approximately 800 species of birds are found in Australia: that is just under 10 per cent of all those in the world. These consist of native, migrant and introduced species. Perhaps only a third of Australia's species are considered common or often sighted on a normal birdwatching trip. Others are only found in specific habitat types, in certain geographical areas or are uncommon to rare or endangered. Migratory species can be divided into regular migrants and vagrants. The regular migrants appear in Australia as part of a regular trip; they travel a set path that can be followed and predicted. Vagrants may only be recorded once or twice in Australia. Since European settlement there have been about 40 introduced species, only about 25 of which have become established. The majority of these were introduced intentionally by humans, while a few birds have managed to introduce themselves.

What Makes a Bird a Bird

When most people are asked to describe the defining characteristic of a bird they immediately say that they fly, but some birds — such as penguins and

emus — do not fly. Also insects and mammals such as bats fly. The next identifying feature they may mention is that birds lay eggs, but so, too, do insects, reptiles and amphibians, fish and some mammals. While both of these characteristics are possessed by some or all of the birds, the only unifying feature is that birds have feathers.

The ground-dwelling Plainswanderer has dull and cryptically patterned plumage.

Birds' feathers are indispensable; they must always be kept in good condition.

Where Birds Live

Birds often have specialised feeding or nesting requirements that are linked to specific environments. Unfortunately widespread destruction of many areas has forced the reduction of a great number of species. Many birds are also limited in range and distribution by weather patterns, limited flight capacity and/or competition. The introduction of feral predators, such as cats, foxes and dingoes, has also forced a retreat by our native species. It is essential that our native habitats are preserved and that wildlife corridors (tracts of native vegetation that allow species to traverse from one area to another) are retained.

Parts of a Bird

Simple things like bill colour may distinguish one species from another, so to make a confident identification, you need to familiarise yourself with the various parts of a bird's body and note their colour, as well as any unusual markings.

WORDS TO KNOW

lores
forehead
upper mandible
crown
eyering
nape
lower mandible
mantle
back
throat
rump
breast
belly
tail

Where Can I Go to See Birds?

Well-watered areas, such as wetlands and swamps, are always good spotting grounds, especially if there is a good walking track close to the waterway. A beach or coastal mudflat is also a good place to look but be sure to check local tide charts so that you do not waste time waiting for the feeding areas to be exposed by the tide. Sitting patiently on a clifftop or taking a boat trip can often be very rewarding, especially when migrating birds, such as albatrosses and shearwaters, are around.

HOMEWORK
If you are hoping to find a particular species, you must first read up on it. It would be a frustrating waste of time and money looking for a bird at one place, only to learn that it has moved north for the winter.

Life on The Edge

The majority of people head for a forest or woodland to see birds. Many of these are protected as national parks and have information areas and easy access via well-maintained walking trails. The best place to look in such habitats is near a clearing or on the fringe of a forest where it overlaps with neighbouring habitats. These areas are often much richer in birdlife than the heart of the forest. Richest of all bird habitats, however, is probably the rain-forests of Australia.

Careful Observation: the Key to Identification

Remember, when you first see a new bird, do not take a few quick looks and then dive straight for the field guide. This will ultimately reveal several similar species, separated by a small detail that you have failed to observe and by the time you look again through the binoculars, the bird has flown, leaving the identification unsolved. Spend time observing every detail and look for unusual markings — this will ultimately save much frustration. The more notes made in the field, the easier and more positive the identification will be later.

Rainforests contain the richest diversity of birds. However, the dimly lit interior can make viewing difficult for birdwatchers.

Albert's Lyrebirds are secretive residents of eastern Australian rainforests.

Basic Essentials

All that you need to go birdwatching is a pair of binoculars, or telescope, a bird guide, a notebook and an idea of where to go and what to look for. This guide offers you the majority of what you will need. Coupled with *A Photographic Guide to Birds of Australia* (see page 97), you should be well prepared.

Adequate clothing is important on a birdwatching trip, too. If your jacket is loose and flaps in the wind, it is more likely to scare the birds away than one that is a little more sturdy. A hat is essential for keeping the sun off your head and face but it is also useful to break up your body's outline, often allowing you to get a little closer to the bird. Good walking shoes are a must and sufficient clothing to allow for changeable weather. A first-aid kit is often wise as birds are not the only animals in the bush; I have often nearly trodden on a snake while gazing up at the treetops. One final thing, if you are going to go out on your own, make sure someone knows where you have gone but tell them not to panic if you are a little late because time flies when you're having fun.

Local birdwatching only requires binoculars, knowledge and patience. Longer trips require more preparation.

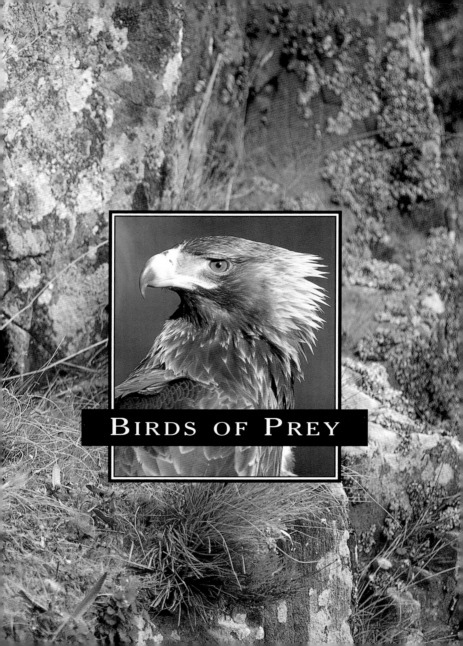

BIRDS OF PREY

Birds of Prey

Found along Australia's and many cosmopolitan coastlines, the Osprey is a keen fish hunter.

All birds of prey have powerful curved bills and long sharp talons. The power, grace and mystique of these magnificent birds is unmistakable each time a sleek Peregrine Falcon darts past or a majestic Wedge-tailed Eagle soars high on huge, 'finger-tipped' wings. Of the roughly 300 species of bird of prey found throughout the world, 25 occur in Australia. Some of these, such as the Osprey, have distributions that extend to many other areas of the world; most, however, are restricted to the Pacific region. A few species, such as the Grey Falcon, are found only in Australia.

NESTING NEIGHBOURS

Some birds, such as the Willie Wagtail, are often found nesting near nesting birds of prey, and occasionally in the nest's base. This association may benefit both species. Strongly territorial, the bird of prey would offer nest protection, while the bold and aggressive Willie Wagtail would be quick to alert the raptor to an intruder's presence.

The Two Major Groups

Birds of prey, or raptors as they are commonly referred to, divide into two groups. The first is the eagles, hawks, harriers and kites; these encompass the majority of Australian raptors: 19 in all. These birds vary in size, wing shape, general appearance and habits. Prey also varies quite widely within the group. The Osprey and White-bellied Sea-Eagle are primarily hunters of fish, although the White-bellied Sea-Eagle will also take birds, mammals, snakes and some carrion. Others, such as the Pacific Baza, target insects as their main source of food.

While this group contains the Black Kite, Australia's and arguably the world's most common bird of prey, the second smaller group, the falcons, contains the rarest: the Grey Falcon, which is found in Australia's lightly timbered arid areas preying upon birds, mammals and insects.

The Black Kite is also known as the Fork-tailed Kite.

Black Kite
47–55cm

This medium-sized dark brown bird of prey is a common sight around bush-fires, where it seizes the unfortunate insects and small animals that flee the flames. Its range covers the majority of the Australian mainland, as well as Europe, Africa and Asia. Its drab plumage makes it sometimes difficult to distinguish from other birds of prey, such as the Little Eagle, Whistling Kite and Square-tailed Kite. In flight, however, its long forked tail and almost unmarked underwing makes it unmistakable.

The Black Kite is found in a wide variety of habitats, from timbered watercourses to open plains and outback towns but it avoids the wetter areas. Sometimes Black Kites form huge flocks of many thousands of birds but they are more often seen in small groups or alone. The call, a whistled 'psee-err' followed by a repeated 'si-si-si', is similar to that of the Whistling Kite.

> **ONE EYE ON THE TIP**
> The Black Kite is a regular visitor to the local tip, where it scavenges. Often gathering in large numbers, it also scavenges on scraps or road kills.

Nankeen Kestrels are commonly seen hovering above their prey.

Nankeen Kestrel
31–36cm

This slightly built falcon is found in most habitats throughout Australia. When observed, its rich rufous upperparts and pale buff underparts, both sparsely spotted and streaked with black, and black-tipped wings and tail, distinguish it from other similar-sized birds of prey.

In open woodland and agricultural areas, where it is most common, the Nankeen Kestrel is often seen hovering a short distance above the ground. By rapidly beating its wings and using its fan-shaped tail as a rudder, it keeps its head and body perfectly still. In this manner it locates the insects, reptiles and small mammals on which it feeds.

Other comparable birds of prey are the similar sized Australian Hobby, 30–35 cm, which has blue-grey upperparts, red-brown underparts and a long, square-shaped tail, and the larger Brown Falcon, 41–51 cm, which lacks the rich rufous colouring. The Nankeen Kestrel nests in a wide variety of sites, including tree hollows, caves and even ledges on the outside of buildings.

How High Can Eagles Fly?

*B*irds of prey, like many other birds, use updrafts of hot air to soar high above the ground. Soaring is used, particularly by the larger birds, to save energy during the long periods that are spent in the air, either migrating or searching for food. The larger birds of prey, such as eagles, buzzards and vultures, are well equipped for soaring on these thermal currents since they have broad wings.

The beautiful White-bellied Sea-Eagle soars over coastal waters as it hunts.

Generally, birds of prey soar at heights of 200 to 1000 metres above the ground while searching for food. During migrations, however, certain species may attain heights of 2000 to 4000 metres and reports of birds at heights of up to 6400 metres are not uncommon. One record of a bird of prey, a Ruppel's Griffon from Africa, was made at 10 000 metres after the bird struck a plane at this altitude. This bird is not even a migrating species so the record is regarded as quite exceptional.

Are Birds of Prey Scared of Other Birds?

*A*ll birds, including birds of prey, are cautious and are constantly on the lookout for dangers and threats to their survival. Occasionally you may see a smaller bird, such as a Willie Wagtail or Magpie-lark, apparently scare off an eagle or another large predator.

Certain species are much more aggressive than others when it comes to protecting their territories and nest sites. This is especially true of many of the

Birds of prey see eight times better than humans.

EAGLE EYES
While soaring at great heights, birds of prey are able to spot the slightest movements of prey on the ground. The visual capacity of these birds has been estimated at possibly more than eight times that of a human being. The muscles that control the curvature of the lens are stronger in these birds than in any other. Also an area of the eye called the pecten, a structure that is attached to the optic nerve, is larger in birds of prey. The pecten is directly linked to the sensitivity of vision.

black and white coloured birds. One or more birds attack the predator and scold it with alarm and threat calls. In most cases the larger predator is unable to catch the smaller, more mobile, attackers and simply flies away, possibly more annoyed than frightened. Pursuers may also peck at the head and wings of predators; if serious damage is done to these parts of the bird, its hunting abilities can be disastrously impaired.

How do Pesticides Affect Birds of Prey?

DDT and other pesticides have caused many bird fatalities, especially among birds of prey.

*T*he introduction of DDT in 1942 and many other associated pesticides has had a dramatic and disastrous effect on many species of birds. Perhaps the most documented effects have been on the Peregrine Falcon.

Pesticides eventually go into the soil, where they become concentrated within the bodies of micro-organisms. This concentration then becomes greater in the animals that feed on these creatures, and their predators concentrate it further. Animals at the top of the food chain, such as birds of prey, may carry pesticides with concentrations up to 5000 times greater than those of the target organisms. Death is the most obvious effect of pesticides but other factors, such as nervous disorders, inability to establish breeding, eggshell thinning and young deformities and mortalities are all associated with pesticides.

ONE BIRD'S POISON
Although harmful to birds, DDT was responsible for saving potentially millions of human lives during the Second World War. At this time it was used to destroy lice that were spreading the typhus virus.

WADERS & WATERBIRDS

Ducks

Of the 21 species of Australian ducks, the Pacific Black Duck is one of the most common.

Within Australia, there are 26 members in this group of partially or fully web-footed birds. Of these, three are vagrants and two are introduced. Although there is only one native swan, the world's only black swan, the introduced Mute Swan is also found here. Three species of geese also occur in Australia: the introduced Canada Goose found on Lord Howe Island, the Cape Barren Goose and the Magpie Goose. This latter species differs from all other members of geese in having only partially webbed toes. Of the remaining 21 species, the more common ones are the Plumed Whistling-Duck, the Australian Wood Duck, the Pacific Black Duck, the Grey Teal, the Chestnut Teal and the Hardhead.

BAD DUCK LUCK
The Musk Duck gets its name from the strong musk odour produced by the male from a gland on the rump. The male Musk Duck also has an unfortunate reputation for being perhaps the most grotesque-looking of all of Australia's birds due to the large fleshy lobe that hangs under its bill.

Feeding Behaviour

Species such as the Musk Duck, Blue-billed Duck, Hardhead, Green Pygmy-goose and Wandering Whistling-Duck obtain some food by diving below the surface of the water. The Plumed Whistling-Duck, Australian Wood Duck, Australian Shelduck, Radjah Shelduck and vagrant Paradise Shelduck are seldom seen in the water, preferring to wade through the shallows or graze in grasslands. The Australian Shoveler, Northern Shoveler and Pink-eared Duck have specialist bills that they use to filter through the water for microscopic aquatic animals and plants. The remaining species follow the more traditional method of upending in the water and feeding on a variety of plants and animals from the bottom of their shallow wetland homes.

Magpie Geese form huge flocks in Australia's north.

Magpie Goose   71–92cm

This large goose is widespread throughout coastal northern and eastern Australia, although some individuals, mostly younger birds, are seen quite long distances inland. Large, noisy flocks of several hundred to a few thousand birds congregate in shallow wetlands, estuaries and wet grasslands, feeding on specific types of aquatic vegetation. A Magpie Goose is unmistakable. The head and neck are black, with a characteristic knobbed crown (larger in males), and the underparts are white, with black margins on the underwing. The bill, legs and feet are orange.

During the breeding season, generally February to June, these birds build nests in secluded places, such as treetops, normally in proximity to wetlands or on floating vegetation. As two females may occasionally use the same nest, the large, oval, off-white coloured eggs may number up to 16 but eight is a more common size. Almost single-handed, the male constructs the nest, but both sexes, and often a second female, will share the incubation duties.

The Black Swan is the world's only black-coloured swan.

Black Swan   117–142cm

Although this species has been introduced to several countries throughout the world, the Black Swan is closely associated with Australia, along with the Emu and Laughing Kookaburra. It can be found on the larger salt, brackish or fresh waterways and in permanent wetlands, where it feeds on algae and weeds.

The Black Swan is aptly named, as it is the only swan in the world that is black in colour, all other species being almost entirely white, except for one South American species that has a black neck. In adult birds, the bill is orange-red with a white line towards the tip. In flight, the neck is held outstretched and the white wingtips are visible. Younger birds are much greyer in colour and have black wingtips. Black Swans require up to 40 metres or more of clear water to take off. Males are larger than females.

Why Don't Ducks Get Wet?

Ducks regularly coat their feathers with a special fatty oil to avoid water saturation.

*D*ucks have a special gland called an oil gland. This gland is found on the rump of the bird, just above the tail. During the normal course of preening — an important process whereby the feathers are arranged, cleaned and generally maintained — the bird squeezes a fatty secretion (preen oil) from the gland using its bill. Both the head and bill are rubbed on the gland, and the oil is then applied evenly to all the feathers by rubbing and preening with the bill, head and feet.

Ducks apply the oil to their feathers frequently, especially during and after bathing. The oil protects the feathers and down from becoming water-logged by creating a film that is not penetrable by the water. The water simply beads into small droplets and runs off the oily surface of the plumage; hence the term 'like water off a duck's back'.

Should I Feed Bread to Ducks?

*P*eople have been feeding bread to ducks for many years and very few of them appear to be adversely affected by this activity; in fact Mallard numbers are higher in areas where they are fed bread. Dry bread, however, may be harmful to birds as it swells up when in contact with water and so may expand inside the bird. Most ducks, however, feed in the water where the bread may already have swollen up but it is wise not to feed birds on land. Pet suppliers provide a special feed for ducks that are kept in captivity and this would always be a better alternative.

It is best to wet bread before feeding it to ducks.

A GOOSEY DUCK
The Australian Wood Duck is also called the Maned Duck or Maned Goose. This name is derived from the short black plumes on the rear of the male's head. The name of goose refers to this bird's upright stance when it walks.

Why is that Duck Perched in a Tree?

Sharp toenails give perching ducks grip.

*P*erhaps the more extraordinary members of the large and widespread duck family are the perching ducks. They are mostly quite different in appearance from one another as well as from other species of duck. As the name suggests, the birds generally spend much of their time in trees. Nesting in tree hollows is common, although certain species do nest on the ground.

In keeping with this lifestyle, their toenails are sharpened. Certain species have enlarged eyes and/or elongated legs and most have wide and rounded wings. The Australian Wood Duck, found in lightly timbered areas adjacent to water-courses, is less of a tree dweller than its relatives, preferring to graze on ground vegetation. During the breeding season, however, suitable nest hollows are sought. If competition for nesting sites is high or their availability low, Wood Ducks may often travel up to a kilometre or more from water. Other Australian members of this group are the pygmy-geese and whistling ducks.

A RANDY DUCK
The common and familiar Mallard is the only introduced duck in Australia to have established in the wild. It has long been famed for its over-active sexual behaviour, with reports of gang attacks on other birds, including roosting owls. It readily interbreeds with other species of duck, such as the Grey and Chestnut Teal.

The randy Mallard is the only introduced duck in Australia to have become established in the wild.

Brolgas construct a large nest of plant stems.

Brolga   110–134cm

This large grey crane, with a red head and grey crown, is widespread across tropical northern Australia, southwards through central New South Wales to western Victoria. Within these areas it can be found in wetlands, coastal mudflats, grasslands, woodlands, crops and, less frequently, mangrove-studded creeks and estuaries.

Although omnivorous (feeding on either vegetable or animal matter), the Brolga prefers to feed on tubers and crops but some insects, molluscs and amphibians are also taken. Within New South Wales, the Brolga's numbers have been much reduced due to widespread draining of its habitats for human activities, such as agriculture, land reclamation and water regulation, but birds are still common and widespread throughout Australia's north.

Another species of crane is also found in Australia. The Sarus Crane, confined to Australia's north, can be identified by its dull pink legs (Brolga's legs are grey), and the red of the head extending down the neck.

This species is also called the Jabiru.

Black-necked Stork   129–137cm

This large bird, with a black and white body, a glossy dark green and purple neck and a robust black bill, is the only member of the stork family found in Australia. It inhabits wetlands, such as floodplains of rivers with large shallow swamps and pools, and deeper permanent bodies of water. Within these areas the Black-necked Stork, or Jabiru, feeds on fish, small crustaceans and amphibians, and uses tall vegetation over deep water for nesting. The female can be identified from the male by its yellow eyes.

The range of this majestic bird has been reduced due to the modification of floodplains and tall reedbeds for agriculture, mining and human settlement. Throughout the monsoonal areas of northern Australia, the Black-necked Stork is still widespread but numbers diminish southwards. In the past the species was found in South Australia, Victoria and much of New South Wales but it is now extinct throughout the majority of these areas.

The robust Purple Swamphen is unmistakable for any other rail.

Purple Swamphen   44–48cm

This large, purplish blue and black rail is unmistakable. Its robust red bill with frontal shield and large orange-red legs and feet are characteristic. Its loud 'kee-ow' call is also distinctive.

The Purple Swamphen is a common sight throughout northern and eastern Australia, where it inhabits freshwater swamps, marshlands and streams. There is also a small isolated population in southwestern Western Australia. Its main diet is the soft shoots of reeds and rushes and small animals, such as frogs and snails, but it is a reputed egg stealer and will eat ducklings if it can catch them. It holds its food firmly with its long toes while consuming it.

Swamphens are generally found in small groups consisting of more males than females. A single female mates with several males and all members share in the incubation and care of the young. For such a bulky bird, the Purple Swamphen is an accomplished flier — birds have transported themselves from Australia to New Guinea and New Zealand.

Eurasian Coots feed almost exclusively on vegetable matter.

Eurasian Coot   32–39cm

Often referred to as the Bald Coot, the Eurasian Coot is an attractive bird. The name Bald Coot stems from the Saxon word bald, meaning white, and refers to its snowy white bill. The remainder of the bird is black, except for its bright red eye. The Coot is found throughout Australia and is common in suitably vegetated lagoons and swamps where it feeds almost entirely on vegetable matter, with a few insects, worms and fish taken to supplement its diet.

This coot is an aggressive bird and because of this it is found in healthy numbers wherever it occurs. During breeding, pairs establish and maintain territories with vigour, announcing themselves with a loud 'kowk', often accompanied by assorted screeches. Their aggression is also extended towards other species and ducks' nests are often used as roosting sites, with the unfortunate owner's eggs being pushed off into the water. The Eurasian Coot has recently transported itself to New Zealand where it is quickly becoming established.

Can Birds Walk on Water?

Sometimes it looks that way. Birds' feet come in many different shapes and sizes and are all well suited to their environment and lifestyle. In most cases the legs are positioned just behind the bird's centre of gravity and the bird's weight is placed on the toes. In certain species of waterbirds the legs and toes are elongated, dispersing their body weight over a

The long spreading toes of this young Jacana make lilypad walking easy.

larger area to facilitate walking on soft ground while searching for food. In the Jacana the toes and claws have become so long that the bird can walk on vegetation lying on the surface of the water, such as waterlilies, in order to pick out small insects and seeds. If casually observed the birds seem indeed to be walking on water and have thereby earned the alternative name of Christbird but another popular name, Lilytrotter, is perhaps more appropriate.

What Makes a Floating Nest Float?

This Australasian Grebe's floating nest remains anchored by fixed plant material.

Floating nests are constructed by certain species of waterbirds to protect their eggs and young in the same way that moats were used to surround castles in medieval times. Birds such as grebes gather masses of floating vegetation and manufacture large pads. These pads are always connected to a plant to prevent the nest from floating away. Jacanas, on the other hand, place only a small amount of material on top of a water-lily leaf. These shallow nests are quite delicate and often the male, who solely looks after the eggs and young birds, has to construct a new nest and transport the eggs and young chicks to it. Certain species of waterbird use reed tussocks for their nests. The reeds are cut and flattened to provide a nesting platform but, although surrounded by water, the nests are not truly floating.

How Much Can a Pelican Hold in its Bill?

*T*here is considerable truth in the popular saying that a pelican can hold more in its bill than it can in its belly. In fact in certain species the large pouched bill, which is regularly stretched to retain its elasticity, can hold more than its entire body weight.

The normal prey of the pelican is fish and occasionally crustaceans. The fish are often herded into a confined area by several pelicans that have formed themselves into a large circle. They tighten the circle to concentrate the density of fish, then submerge their heads in the water and fill their bills with both water and fish. They expel the water from their bills using their tongues and swallow the fish by tilting their heads back.

The bill is capable of holding up to 14 litres of water as well as a quantity of fish. Fish extracted from the bill of one young bird weighed 4 kg, nearly half of its body weight, and an adult bird returning to its nest was found to have almost the same. Given that a litre of water weighs approximately one kilogram, and that an average catch of fish was one kilogram, a pelican may hold up to 15 kg in its bill. The largest species of pelican is the Dalmatian Pelican, native to Europe and Asia, which weighs a maximum of 13 kg.

UNUSUAL FOOD FOR A BIRD

Pelicans have been well documented for catching and often eating unusual things. The larger species of pelican have been recorded catching and eating small dogs and there is also one record of a pelican grabbing a young child in its bill before the parents forced the bird to let go. Less dramatic but just as interesting is the Australian Pelican which is well renowned for eating ducks and their young.

Pelicans have an enormous pouched bill that they use for catching quantities of fish and some less likely foods.

Cormorants

Like all cormorants, the Pied Cormorant resembles the closely related Darter (inset), which is hanging its wings out to dry.

Cormorants are medium to large birds that are skilled underwater fishers. All have long slender bodies and necks, short stiff tails, webbed feet, and slender bills with a pronounced hooked tip. The closely related Darter, while superficially similar, has a pointed bill and a long snake-like neck.

Australia's Cormorants

The Great, Pied, Little Pied and Little Black Cormorants are the most common and can be seen throughout Australia. The Little Pied Cormorant, 50–60 cm, is found in almost any body of fresh or salt water. It is entirely black above and white below. The larger, 65–80 cm, Pied Cormorant resembles the Little Pied Cormorant but has a bright yellow-orange face. These colonial nesters breed when fish, crustaceans and molluscs are plentiful.

The Little Black Cormorant, 60–65 cm, is entirely black in plumage. It prefers fresh water and is a familiar sight on farm dams but it also inhabits salted waterways. The Great Cormorant, 70–90 cm, is one of the largest cormorants in the world. Its black plumage is punctuated only by a white chin and yellow throat.

The Black-faced Cormorant, 60–70 cm, looks like a Pied Cormorant but has a black face. The Imperial Shag, 70–75 cm, black above and white below, is unmistakable within its range of Australia's Antarctic islands.

> **HANGING OUT**
> The plumage of the cormorants and darters is not particularly waterproof and birds are often seen with their wings held open, 'hung out to dry'. Due to this limitation cormorants generally only take to the water when hunting.

The secretive Australian Spotted Crake.

Australian Spotted Crake 18–21cm

Found in thickly vegetated lagoons and swamplands, this large crake is distinguished from others by its all-white undertail and two-tone olive green and red bill. The upperparts are mottled brown and black, spotted with white, and its underparts are barred black and white with a blue-grey breast.

Inhabiting both eastern and western Australia, the Australian Spotted Crake is somewhat of a nomad. Although it is normally found in coastal areas, it suddenly appears in inland areas, only to disappear as mysteriously and suddenly as it arrived.

As with most crakes, this is a relatively shy bird, darting backwards and forwards in search of food, insects, molluscs and aquatic plants, or skulking in the shadows. Although common, these secretive habits make it difficult to see but patience is often rewarded with good glimpses of birds as they forage in the mud or shallow water, apparently oblivious to the presence of a quiet observer.

A breeding Hoary-headed Grebe.

Hoary-headed Grebe 27–30cm

Commonly seen, but often mistaken for the Australasian Grebe, the Hoary-headed Grebe is perhaps the most gregarious of the three grebes in Australia. It is often seen nesting and roosting in groups.

It is found on open fresh or brackish waterways throughout most of Australia. The Hoary-headed Grebe is most easily identified during the breeding season, typically October to March but it may breed at any time in response to rainfall. At such times it has generally grey upperparts, white underparts, a black throat and dark grey head, streaked by numerous overlying white plumes. At other times the head loses its long plumes, the crown becomes blackish and the throat white.

When sighted, the Hoary-headed Grebe seldom allows a close approach, generally taking to the air with rapid flight. The Australasian Grebe, on the other hand, tends to dive beneath the surface of the water, rarely taking to the air during the daylight hours. Grebes are adept fishers; they catch small fish, aquatic invertebrates and other insects in skilful underwater pursuits.

Why do Waterbirds Have Funny-shaped Bills?

*T*he shape of a bird's bill varies according to its feeding behaviour. Mergansers, a type of duck, have serrated bills specially adapted to grasping fish. The long, pointed bills found in herons, egrets and bitterns are used for quickly seizing fast-moving prey. Waders have elongated bills for probing the mud in search of food and then piercing or levering open the hinges of hard shells. Flamingoes have downwardly curved bills with special sieve-like plates, called lamellae, to filter food from

Spoonbills use their sensitive bills to search for food.

the mud. Certain ducks, geese and swans also have these sieve-like devices for filtering food. Avocets have scythe-like bills for skimming aquatic insects and their larvae from the surface of the water, while spoonbills have large spatula-shaped bills that they sweep through the water in an arc of 180 degrees; prey is detected by touch at the wide 'spoon' end of the bill and is quickly seized.

Why do Birds Migrate?

*M*igration is the movement of birds at only known times and in known directions, so it is different from nomadic flights and dispersal. During these trips the birds follow recognised and established routes but they are not necessarily the same in both directions. Basically, migration is a strategy for

increasing a bird's chances of raising young. A bird that takes advantage of suitable breeding climate in two places rather than just one may raise more young. Alternatively a bird may migrate to a warmer climate for the winter or because of a greater abundance of food or daylight

Migrating birds move between breeding and feeding grounds.

Prior to migration, birds store large amounts of fat, to provide energy for their long, exhausting flight.

hours, factors that can increase chances of survival and successfully breeding. Certain areas may contain fewer predators than others and so provide better breeding areas; this is particularly so for birds that moult while breeding as they are especially vulnerable.

WING SPURS

Certain birds have bony projections on their wings called 'spurs'. These are covered with a sheath and are used in combat. The Comb-crested Jacana and the Masked Lapwing are two Australian species that have spurs on their wings.

The Masked Lapwing is armed for combat.

The Hazards of Migration

All of these factors are essentially linked to the increased chances of survival of both individuals and the species as a whole. There are, however, many hazards associated with migration. In most species migration uses high amounts of energy. Birds derive this energy from fat that builds up throughout their bodies, especially under the skin, prior to the journey. These 'fat pads', as they are collectively termed, may increase the bird's body weight by 50 per cent. The total fat reserve is directly related to the distance that the bird must travel. Those undergoing migration in a series of short hops need less than those doing a single, long migratory flight. If unforeseen weather conditions prevail during the migration or if birds do not build up sufficient fat reserves for the flight, they are likely to run out of energy and die of starvation.

Waders

Some waders, such as this elegant Black-winged Stilt, have long legs and bills for wading and feeding in the shallows; others, like this juvenile Sharp-tailed Sandpiper (inset) feed along shores.

Waders is a loose term used for birds associated with watery areas, especially salty ones. Avocets, stilts, sandpipers and curlews, which are generally found along the shores and inland waterways, are all waders. Another commonly used term for waders is shorebirds.

Approximately 70 species of waders may be seen in Australia; most are migratory and many are reputed for the spectacularly long journeys they make. Some, however, are residents and they can be found at any time of the year. The Bush Stone-curlew and Beach Stone-curlew, for example, are rather bizarre long-legged birds with cryptic plumage. The Bush Stone-curlew may be found considerable distances inland but it is still related to the wader group.

Waders are most easily viewed on the water's edge during low tide. Here they run quickly backwards and forwards, frantically collecting food or busily probing the soft ground for submerged animals.

Now You See Me...

Many wader species are frustratingly similar and often difficult to tell apart. Found mostly in large numbers, they are very wary of intruders, seldom allowing a close approach. Many of those recorded in Australia have been classed as vagrants. This means that they are not regular visitors. They turn up on rare occasions, perhaps when they have been blown off course or become lost.

Bar-tailed Godwit: a non-breeding migrant.

Bar-tailed Godwit 37–45cm

This bird is a common sight throughout coastal Australia during August to April each year. A non-breeding migrant, the Bar-tailed Godwit can be identified by its large size and long, slightly upturned bill. It is often difficult to distinguish it from the similar Black-tailed Godwit but its white underwing, barred rump, shorter bill and lack of white wingbar should identify it when the two are compared.

Godwits are found in large groups, busily probing the sand or mud in estuarine mudflats, beaches and mangroves for molluscs, worms and aquatic insects. They are often seen in the company of other waders. The Bar-tailed Godwit breeds each year in Scandinavia, northern Asia and Alaska, and winters in Australia, New Zealand and Africa. Although the majority of the birds will return to their breeding grounds in April, some may remain all year round. These are most probably immature birds.

Black-fronted Dotterels feed at the water's edge.

Black-fronted Dotterel 16–18cm

This small wader is a breeding resident in Australia. When observed it is easily identified by its white under-parts and distinct black Y-shaped band which extends across the chest, around to the base of the neck and through the eye to the forehead. This may be absent in younger birds. Its bill is orange-red, tipped with black, and it has a conspicuous orange ring around the eye.

The Black-fronted Dotterel is common throughout the Australian mainland and Tasmania. It inhabits the margins of lakes, swamps and dams, where it feeds on insects, crustaceans and some seeds. Usually found in pairs or small groups, it is an active feeder but its cryptic mottled brown and black upperparts provide excellent camouflage when nesting or at rest. The two to three eggs, laid in a simple shallow scrape in the ground, are cared for by both sexes. The young chicks are also well camouflaged but if threatened the adults will feign injury in attempt to distract the predator away from the nest. This tactic is a common ploy among ground-nesters and most especially among waders.

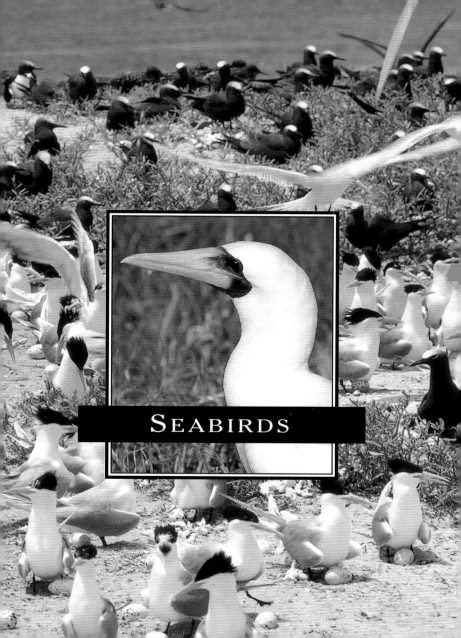

SEABIRDS

Petrels and Shearwaters

Ocean-flying petrels and shearwaters, such as this Wedge-tailed Shearwater, spend lengthy periods at sea.

Within Australia, this group consists of about 50 species. All members are ocean-dwelling birds associated with the temperate and cooler oceans.

Prions and Shearwaters

Prions are small dove-like birds. All are blue-grey above with a black M-shaped line visible in flight and white below. The shearwaters are all dark brown or dark brown and white and have long, slender bills.

Giant-petrels, Fulmars and Petrels

Giant-petrels are large brown and white albatross-like birds. They are active scavengers of carrion and refuse. The Southern Fulmar is large (45–50 cm) and gull-like. It is the only light grey and white coloured petrel found in the Southern Hemisphere. The petrels are an assortment of birds that vary widely in size and coloration but are characteristic of the colder Arctic and Antarctic areas.

> **'UNEMPLOYED' BUT INTEGRATED**
> Petrels and shear-waters breed in large colonies on islands. For many reasons, such as sickness, injury or inability to find a mate, some birds may not breed but they still remain with the colony. These birds are termed 'unemployed'.

Storm-petrels and Diving-petrels

The storm-petrels are distinct from other petrels and shearwaters by being much smaller, having grey, black and white plumage and long legs. They also perform a spectacular dancing flight on the surface of the water as they search for food. The diving-petrels are restricted to the cooler waters of the Southern Hemisphere. Their plumage is black above and white below, and their short, narrow wings are specially adapted to diving for food.

Perhaps the most famous seabird, a Wandering Albatross may have a wingspan over three metres.

Wandering Albatross 80–135cm

No other species of bird has gained so much admiration and respect from birdwatchers and fishermen alike. The Wandering Albatross may spend days following a ship, gliding effortlessly on long slender wings in all but the calmest winds. It is distinguished by its large size and white plumage marked with fine black wavy lines on the breast, neck and upper back, and mottled with black on the back.

Birds will readily scavenge from fishing boats and the surface of the water but squid and fish are its preferred food. This penchant for squid has put the bird at risk from the longlines used by ocean trawlers. The albatross becomes hooked and drowns as it takes the bait.

The Wandering Albatross breeds on subantarctic islands from early December. The chicks, which are often abandoned for long periods as their parents search for food, remain in the nest for approximately eight to nine months.

Little Penguins spend much time at sea, waiting for the cover of night before returning to land.

Little Penguin 32–34cm

This small, blue and white penguin is a common sight along the coastline of southern Australia from Perth, Western Australia, to about Nelson Bay, New South Wales. Spending the daylight hours at sea, it awaits the cover of night before coming ashore to roost in rock crevices and burrows.

The Little or Fairy Penguin is the only species of penguin to nest on the Australian mainland. On Phillip Island, Victoria, the nightly 'penguin parades' have become a tourist attraction and ferry travellers in Sydney are often delighted with a view of a penguin resting on the surface of the water in the Harbour.

Like other penguins, it catches its food, mostly small fish and squid, by skilful underwater pursuits. The bird flaps its wings as it swims, as if it were 'flying' underwater. Unfortunately Little Penguins have suffered over the years as a result of predation by Feral Cats and Foxes, and due to disturbance by humans; colony sizes have been reduced by over a third of their original numbers.

How Far and Fast do Seabirds Fly?

Seabirds spend almost their entire lives at sea and are accomplished fliers; they able to ride ocean winds and battle through stormy weather. In order to find enough food, they must cover vast areas of ocean and in relatively short periods of time. As a general rule, birds in their first year tend to be more nomadic and travel greater distances than older ones. While few records are available as to the exact time a bird spends at sea, it is the speed and distances they travel that are perhaps most impressive.

Seabirds travel vast distances as regular migrants or in their search for food.

Some Record-breakers

The Wandering Albatross has long slender wings with a span greater than any other bird — up to 3.5 m in full-grown birds. It has been recorded flying almost 6000 km in 12 days. During the eight or nine months that a parental Wandering Albatross has young in the nest, at least one parent is more or less permanently at sea searching for food for the family while the other babysits.

The record-breaker, at least on a daily basis, however, presently goes to the Manx Shearwater, one of which is known to have travelled some 9500 km in just 17 days. Other species of seabird are known to undertake extensive migrations across the seas. These are not fishing trips but true migrations. One of the best known seabird migrations is that of the Great Shearwater; this bird is known to spend almost nine months continuously on the wing as it travels from a group of islands called Tristan da Cunha to off the coast of Newfoundland.

How Long Can a Penguin Hold its Breath?

Penguins are proficient swimmers. At sea they appear graceful as they torpedo through the water in pursuit of food or to escape from a predator. The penguin steers its streamlined body through the water with the aid of its feet and short tail. It can reach speeds of more than 12 km per hour, although 8 km per hour is more usual.

Most penguins dive to

Penguins rest on the surface with outstretched wings.

depths of less than 100 metres; the Little Penguin normally dives to about 70 metres. The Emperor Penguin is the largest of the penguins; it has been recorded at depths greater than 540 metres. These enormous dives are made possible by huge oxygen reserves which allow the bird to stay underwater for periods in excess of 18 minutes.

Who Killed all These Birds on the Beach?

Many muttonbirds die of starvation during their long migration.

*T*hese dark brown birds with rounded tails and long, dark grey legs and feet are Short-tailed Shearwaters, or Muttonbirds. Each year during October and November vast flocks of Muttonbirds make their way down from their wintering grounds in the northern Pacific and Antarctic region to the breeding colonies off the south and southeastern coasts of Australia.

Due to exhaustion, sickness and bad weather an enormous number of dead and dying birds are washed up on our beaches at this time of year. Although this may appear alarming at first, a vast number of birds make this annual migration. Breeding colonies off the coast of Tasmania total upwards of 16 million adults and other colonies in Victoria and New South Wales add a further 2 million or more birds.

HARVESTING

Each year, between 27 March and 30 April, large numbers of Muttonbirds are harvested in Bass Strait. The young birds are taken, their oily stomach contents refined for use in the pharmaceutical industry and their bodies cleaned and sold for food. Strict control measures regulate the harvesting of the birds to ensure that overall population numbers are not threatened.

Gulls & Terns

These immature Pacific Gulls seldom venture far from land.
Inset: A White-capped noddy nesting on Heron Island.

*T*he gulls and terns, and the related skuas and jaegers, have approximately 35 representatives in Australia, although several are rare vagrants. Typically, gulls are white below, with light grey to grey-black wings and back; some have black hoods. The Pacific, Kelp and Silver Gulls are Australian residents. The Silver Gull is perhaps the most common and widespread, while both the Kelp and Pacific Gulls are restricted to Australia's southern coasts. Terns are similarly coloured and in both groups males and females are virtually identical.

Closely related to the gulls and terns are the noddys. These birds have long slender bills and uniformly coloured plumage. They are generally found in open marine areas and breed on offshore islands.

Thieves and Pirates

The skuas and jaegers are all strongly migratory and, as such, may appear close to the mainland from time to time. Essentially, however, they are found on arctic and antarctic islands. The skuas are thieves of eggs and nestlings, which they take from unattended nests. They will also take adult birds and scavenge on carcasses. The jaegers are the 'pirates' of the sea, relentlessly hounding smaller birds until they regurgitate their food which is caught in flight by the jaegers. They also take small birds and mammals.

> ### NAMES WITH MEANING
> There are six species of skuas and jaegers. The group is found at both polar regions. The name 'skua' is derived from their Icelandic name, 'skufr', which describes their shrieking call. 'Jaeger' is German in origin and translates as 'hunter'.

Silver Gull 40–45cm

The Silver Gull is Australia's most common gull.

This is the smallest of the resident Australian gulls. In adult birds the plumage is grey above with a white head, neck and underparts; younger birds have varying amounts of brown mottling on the back and wings. Adult birds also differ from the young in having conspicuous red-orange legs, bills and eyerings; these are black to brown in younger birds.

The Silver Gull is common and widespread and is found near virtually any watery area. While it may be observed at great distances inland, it seldom ventures far out to sea although birds will flock in high numbers around fishing boats as they leave or return to the coast. Besides its Australian distribution, the species is also found in New Zealand and New Caledonia. As with many other gull species, the Silver Gull has adapted successful to human activities and readily begs for handouts of food scraps.

Crested Tern 44–49cm

A yellowish bill identifies the Crested Tern.

In coastal areas this medium-sized tern, with its robust yellow bill, grey wings and back, white neck and underparts, and scraggy black crest, is perhaps the most commonly seen tern in Australia. It is the second largest Australian species of tern; the first, the Caspian Tern, measures 50 to 55 cm and has a huge red bill. The similar Lesser Crested Tern, found in northern Australia, has an orange bill and a more extensive black crest.

The Crested Tern feeds mainly on fish, which it catches by plunging into the sea in a typical tern manner. Often observed in large mixed flocks with other terns or gulls, the Crested Tern is highly gregarious. Breeding takes place between October and December each year in large, noisy colonies on offshore islands. The eggs, placed in a shallow scrape in the ground, are incubated by both sexes and both care for the young.

Do Seagulls Prefer Chips to Fish?

*A*s with most seagulls, Silver Gulls often gather in vast numbers wherever there is a chance of an easy meal. Although the normal diet is varied, ranging from worms and insects to fish, the Silver Gull will readily take human food and refuse. Due to this adaptability, large numbers of birds often congregate in coastal areas where fast food, particularly fish and chips, are sold. Purchasers of the food are pestered, often

Gulls are expert scavengers and readily accept free handouts.

aggressively, for a handout. Such behaviour has become a major part of the feeding habits of seagulls, most probably because they favour an easy meal, rather than a preference for hot chips.

Why do Gulls Bother Pilots?

*G*ulls are a major pest around airports. They can get sucked into jet engines or even smash into the windscreens of moving planes. Large numbers of Silver Gulls fly across the runways of Sydney Airport at dawn and dusk as they move between roost sites and local feeding grounds. These movements also occur before and after low tide.

This problem is not limited to Sydney. Airports are often built on the outskirts of cities where rubbish tips proliferate and adjacent to large bodies of water. Due to the gulls' association with waterways and rubbish tips they often gather in large numbers in these areas. In Sydney the numbers of birds near the airport have been reduced by moving one tip and changing the hours of operation of another to the night time.

Where airports are close to the ocean, seagulls often become a major hazard.

SEAGULL DETERRENTS
Many methods have been used to deter birds from airports. These include: trapping birds and releasing them away from the airport, repellent gels, moth balls, recorded sounds of predators, flashing lights attached to aircraft, coloured smoke, model aircraft, trained hawks and even regular bursts from claxon horns.

Do Seabirds Get Lost at Sea?

*M*any sightings of vagrant seabirds can be explained as birds that have been blown off course or been forced to land due to particularly bad weather but whether they are really lost is another matter. It appears that birds use many means of navigation, including the sun, the stars, the Earth's magnetic field, visual landmarks, such as islands, and internal programming. In what proportion these factors are used by different birds is uncertain.

Seabirds drink saltwater: excess salt is excreted via a special gland.

SALT GLANDS

Seabirds have a special gland called a salt gland that is able to extract excess salt from their body fluids. Because of this they are able to drink brackish and salt water but, given the choice, they appear to favour fresh water.

One thing that definitely is known is that seabirds can locate their nest by smell, flying downwind of the colony and then following the scent back upwind. This is perhaps why many of them have tube-shaped appendages on their upper mandibles.

Experiments have been carried out on birds' abilities to return to their site of capture after being transported quite a distance to an unfamiliar release site. Of the species tested, most had a greater than 50 per cent success rate; some, such as the Manx Shearwater and Herring Gull, returned a 90 per cent success rate with a distance of up to 1500 km to navigate.

Seabirds seem to navigate by coordinating a number of different natural influences.

SONGBIRDS

Why do Birds Sing?

*B*irds produce sound through a special apparatus called a syrinx, a structure that occurs at the point where the trachea divides into two. The syrinx is only found in birds and is equivalent to our voice box.

Birds emit two types of sounds: calls and songs. Calls are generally regarded as short, simple noises that may be produced by either sex and at any time. Songs, on the other hand, are longer, more complex vocalisations. Songs are normally only given by the male but in many species females sing too.

Song is considered to serve several purposes; it may be proclaiming identity, conveying territory information or attract-

A songbird's syrinx is equivalent to a human's voice box.

ing mates. Which of these is the primary function we still do not know. Field observations and experiments have produced information that reinforces the importance of each so debate will probably continue for many years to come.

Singles Sing More

Some birds have more than one song or even a long and short version of a particular song. The longer version is uttered by unmated birds; once a mate is obtained, the song is shortened. In a species that

contained both polygamous and monogamous males, the polygamous males had a shorter song. This reinforces the notion that long-winded birds are single while those with a partner are much quieter — a fact that is not necessarily confined to our feathered friends.

Bird songs are complex and used for identification, territory announcements or mate attraction.

SONGSTER UNDER SCRUTINY

After a long-term European study of the Sedge Warbler's song, which comprises some fifty notes uttered in often complex arrangements, it was suggested that all that effort could really serve no other purpose but to attract a member of the opposite sex.

What can Birds Mimic & Why?

Certain birds have become well renowned for their ability to mimic. Some unusual sounds that feature in mimicry are: barking dogs, chopping wood, whipcracks, tractor noises, twanging wire, squeaking gates and chainsaws.

In Australia, the bowerbirds, scrub-birds and lyrebirds are the most reputed mimics. A Superb Lyrebird in Taronga Zoo, Sydney, would imitate the sound of a bus as it

The Superb Lyrebird is a great songster of the Australian bush.

changed gear going up the hill outside the zoo, while a semi-domesticated lyrebird on a farm could imitate any of the sounds associated with the yard, including the horse and cart, squealing pigs and the phrases used by the farmer. About 80 per cent of a Superb Lyrebird's song consists of mimicry. It does not have a specific song of its own but it does emit a series of whistles and cackling notes that are thought to be its own.

The Mystery of Mimicry

Why birds mimic has been debated for many years. One explanation is that mimicry is used to supplement the bird's relatively drab plumage, as the best mimics tend to be dull-coloured birds; another is that mimicry may be used as a form of identification between mated pairs. Some scientists have declared that birds do not really mimic at all, rather the sounds accidentally resemble other sounds, or that young birds, when they are learning their own songs, are influenced by nearby species.

The Regent Bowerbird mimics a variety of natural and man-made sounds.

A VARIED REPERTOIRE
Bowerbirds are renowned for their mimicry, and are adept at imitating machinery, crumpling paper, sawing or chopping wood, squeaky gates, cracking stockwhips and natural sounds, such as barking dogs and the calls of other birds.

The Variegated Fairy-wren is widespread.

Variegated Fairy-wren   12–14cm

Only the male of this species bears the bright blue, purple, chestnut, black and white plumage. Females and young birds are brownish to pale blue-grey in colour. The depth and variety of colours in the males vary among the four subspecies scattered throughout the Australian mainland.

The Variegated Fairy-wren is found in a variety of habitats, ranging from heath-lands in the east to arid scrublands in central Australia and rocky ridges in the north. This is the most widespread of the nine Australian species of fairy-wren.

Like most other fairy-wrens, the Variegated Fairy-wren is normally seen in small family groups of up to seven birds. These groups usually consist of a dominant male and female and several young birds that resemble the female in plumage colour. Contrary to popular belief, the brightly coloured male does not have a harem of females; the brown birds are mostly males, as the parental female drives away other females at the onset of the breeding season.

A Striated Pardalote in its tree-hollow nest.

Striated Pardalote   9.5–11cm

Throughout most of the year it is the sharp 'tchip tchip' call of this brightly coloured little bird that often first alerts us to its presence. The Striated Pardalote, like other pardalotes, feeds on arthropods, which it gleans from foliage high up it the tops of trees. When breeding, however, the birds are often much more noticeable as they mostly construct their nests close to the ground, usually in a tree hollow or a tunnel excavated in an earthen bank.

At this time the black crown, white eyebrows with a yellow spot, olive-grey back, black wings with a white stripe and yellow-white underparts are conspicuous. Considerable variations in plumage are found within the range of this species, which extends throughout the eucalypt forests and woodlands of Australia. The black crown may be plain or have fine white stripes and there may be a yellow or red spot at the front end of the white wing stripe.

The White-browed Scrubwren is bold.

White-browed Scrubwren 11–13cm

The White-browed Scrubwren is a noisy and inquisitive bird. Within Australia there are five species of scrubwren, of which this species is the most common and widespread. Its range extends from northern Queensland in a broad coastal band through South Australia to the mid-Western Australian coast and Tasmania. Throughout this range it is found in rainforests, open forests, woodlands, scrublands and heaths.

The White-browed Scrubwren shows some variation in plumage markings and coloration. Predominantly birds are fuscous brown with slightly paler underparts and a characteristic white eyebrow. Birds in Australia's north are more yellow underneath and the males have an almost black facial mask, whereas birds found along the southern coastline have conspicuous dark streaking on the throat.

The White-browed Scrubwren is insectivorous and busily feeds in pairs amongst the thick vegetation of the forest floor. Its call is a repetitive chattering, especially when disturbed, and some mimicry.

The Eastern Yellow Robin's call is 'chop chop'

Eastern Yellow Robin 15–17cm

The Eastern Yellow Robin is a delight to observe in its wide choice of habitat types, mostly dry woodlands and rainforests as well as parks and gardens. It is a medium-sized bird with a grey back and head and yellow underparts. Usually first seen perched on the side of a tree trunk about a metre or so above the ground, it watches the leaf litter below for invertebrate activity. If it spies something that looks like food, it drops to the ground, only staying as long as it takes to pluck the morsel out. It then returns to its perch.

This bird will readily approach humans, often accepting handouts of food from picnickers. Its tameness has made it familiar and it can be easily persuaded to venture near if you make a squeaking noise with your lips and hand.

The call of the Eastern Yellow Robin is an assortment of high bell-like piping, some harsh scolding notes and a repeated 'chop chop'. The superficially similar Pale Yellow Robin is comparatively smaller, has pale lores and lighter underparts.

45

What is That Little Brown Bird?

*P*erhaps the most frustrating birds to identify are those little brown birds that flit around in the tops of tall trees or scurry among the dense vegetation of the darkened forest floor. In birdwatching circles these birds are affectionately called Little Brown Birds or LBBs.

There are several clues to telling these LBBs apart and a quick good glimpse of them is often all that is needed to identify them. Many LBBs are distinguished by small

A Buff-rumped Thornbill has typical thornbill facial marks.

unnoticed characters, for example the presence or absence of striations on the face and throat. In addition the colour of the eye, leg or rump, or markings on the wings and tail may be important.

Geographical distribution is another means of further pinpointing a bird's identity, as is its call. Try and familiarise yourself with the LBBs in the area that you are visiting and the differences in their calls before you go. Habitat and feeding habits are other useful identification factors. Most species are adapted to specific habitats and to more or less specific food, so take note of what that LBB is doing and where. For example, is it feeding in the leaf litter of a rainforest or catching flying insects in open country?

Australia's smallest bird, the Weebill, is found throughout the country.

SMALLEST BIRD

At 8 to 9cm, the Weebill is Australia's shortest bird, particular the ones found in northern Australia where individuals are slightly smaller than those in the south. Some people may argue that the Mallee Emu-wren is the smallest, having a body size of 5 to 6 cm, but its long filamentous tail adds a further 8 to 9 cm to its length.

Do Honeyeaters Only Eat Honey?

*T*he many members of this large family of birds are well known for probing their long downwardly curved bills into flowers and using their brush-tipped tongues to lap up the rich nectar that is hidden deep inside. The lapping action of the tongue is quite rapid — up to ten laps per second.

An Eastern Spinebill lapping up nectar with its tongue.

In most species nectar forms the bulk of a honeyeater's diet. Certain species, however, have a penchant for fruits and berries, particularly the rainforest species, and this has made them somewhat of a pest around commercial orchards. Insects are also taken to supplement the diet in many species, especially around the time when hungry chicks are demanding an ever constant source of food. At such times insects are quite plentiful and are a good source of protein, both for the rapidly growing chicks and the adult birds. In particular many honeyeaters seek out insects called psyllids or lerps and scale insects; these feed on the sap of trees and produce sugary secretions that the honeyeaters find irresistible.

Which Bird is the Bellbird?

The Bell Miner is often called the Bellbird.

A walk through an open forest or woodland will often be accompanied by a beautiful ringing bell-like 'tink' from the Bell Miner. This plump honeyeater with long sharp claws (nicknamed the Pin Cushion Bird in bird-banding circles) is often called the Bellbird.

The Crested Bellbird, formerly called the Oreoica, is found in the arid inland and coastal scrublands of Australia. It is not related to the Bell Miner at all; it is a member of the whistler family that includes the shrike-tit and the shrike-thrushes. While the calls of both birds have a beautiful bell-like quality, that of the Crested Bellbird is more like the sound of a cowbell — an almost ventriloquial noise that has been described as 'pan pan panella'. While bellbird may be quite an apt name for either species, the Crested Bellbird is the rightful owner.

Honeyeaters

*T*his family of predominantly nectar-feeding birds is widespread throughout Australasia, to New Zealand in the south, the Philippines in the north and east to Hawaii. Of the approximately 173 species that are known, 67 occur in Australia. In spite of this relatively extensive distribution, many species are seriously endangered. Land clearance, the introduction of feral animals and the planting of non-native trees have been the three main contributory factors.

Recent research has suggested that the chats are closely related to the honeyeaters, although their habits and physical appearance are somewhat different. For the sake of simplicity, we will only discuss the honeyeaters in this section.

The habits of the honeyeaters can vary considerably from species to species. Certain species, such as the Regent Honeyeater, are migratory. This bird moves northwards in the autumn and winter and returns to breed in southern areas in spring. Most of the species, however, remain in the same area all year round.

Above: a Yellow-tufted Honeyeater.
Right: A Blue-faced Honeyeater.

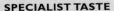

SPECIALIST TASTE
Certain honeyeaters feed exclusively on one plant, and follow its flowering patterns through different areas. The Painted Honeyeater of eastern and northern Australia, for example, feeds mostly on mistletoe, although it has been known to take insects, normally those associated with the mistletoe.

Pollen-eaters or Pollinators?

Superficially, honeyeaters are identified by the size, length and shape of their downwardly curving bills which they probe into flowers to reach nectar, a honey-like fluid found in the base. The tongue tip consists of a series of fibrous hairs that when dipped into the nectar soak up the fluid like a sponge. This feeding behaviour also benefits plants since pollen is distributed by the birds as they move from plant to plant.

The territorial Red Wattlebird.

Red Wattlebird
33.5–36cm

Wattlebirds are the largest of the Australian honeyeaters. Although the Yellow Wattlebird, found only in Tasmania, is the largest of all, the Red Wattlebird comes second, along with two species of friarbird. The Red Wattlebird gets its name from a fleshy reddish wattle on either side of its neck. This is found only in this species, although it is often difficult to see. Besides this, the bird can be identified by its grey-brown body, boldly streaked with white, its yellow belly and long, white-tipped tail. The smaller Little Wattlebird is somewhat similar in plumage but lacks the facial wattles and has conspicuous rufous patches on the undersurface of the wings.

The Red Wattlebird is found in southern areas of the Australian mainland where it inhabits forests, woodlands and gardens; in such areas it aggressively protects the food-bearing plants from other honeyeater species. Its call is a distinctive and loud 'chok' or harsh 'yac a yac'.

The familiar White-plumed Honeyeater.

White-plumed Honeyeater 15–17cm

This honeyeater is common and familiar in most parts of the Australian mainland. Although the intensity of the overall coloration may change slightly throughout its wide range, it is predominantly olive-grey on the body with a paler yellow-olive face. Its name is derived from a conspicuous white line at the base of the cheek that is edged with black. The bill is black when breeding, which may be at any time of the year, and dusky with a yellow base at other times.

Its preference for open habitats has lead to the species being a familiar sight in urban parks and gardens, where it readily feeds on introduced plant species. In more natural areas, it is found in woodlands, especially favouring those adjacent to watercourses. The White-plumed Honeyeater is generally seen in small groups that move busily through the canopy, feeding on a variety of insects, spiders, berries and honeydew (a sugary secretion produced by nectar-feeding insects). The voice is a repetitive 'chickawee'.

What's in a Name?

*I*n Sweden there is a saying: 'God made the plants and animals, Linnaeus named them'. Carl Linnaeus (1707–1778) promoted a system called the Binominal System, which is used today as the basis for applying scientific or Latin names to plants and animals. Although Linnaeus cannot be awarded with all the credit for all the names that have been given to the millions of plants and animals that are known to science, he certainly can be credited for creating the system that is used to do so.

The majority of these names are derived from Latin and Greek and describe a habit or physical

Superficially resembling the European Robin, Australia's Red-capped Robin is in fact not related.

characteristic of the species in question. Others are, however, taken from sources such as mythology, names of prominent people, or are simply an anagram of the bird's popular name or nickname.

Common Names

Along with the scientific name, birds are attributed with a common or English name, or indeed sometimes several names. In Australia, the common name has often been derived from those of British birds, such as the wren, chough and robin. This can be quite misleading as, in many cases, the birds are not in any way related to their namesakes. The common name of a species may also be derived from a word used by local indigenous people, although, in most cases, this name is only used as an alternative to another, more anglicised, name.

Laughing Kookaburra calls are a familiar sound in the Australian bush.

DAWN CHORUS

The Laughing Kookaburra's call is a raucous and prominent part of the dawn chorus. In outback areas this early morning wake-up call gave the bird the names of Bushman's Clock, Alarm Bird and Breakfast Bird.

Origins of Some Bird Names

The name kingfisher is European in origin and is derived from the bird's royal blue and purple plumage and its skilled fishing ability. Both of these characteristics are not found in all species. For example, the kookaburra is a member of the kingfisher family but it rarely, if ever, takes fish as part of its diet.

Three out of four species of Australian birds of paradise are known as riflebirds. The name 'riflebird' is thought to have originated from when the first specimen of the Paradise Riflebird was shot in 1824 by a soldier at Port Macquarie in New South Wales.

Some of the more unusual common bird names include: Guinea-a-week for the Pilotbird; Scissors Grinder for the Restless Flycatcher; Laughing Jackass for the Laughing Kookaburra; Cranky Fan for the Grey Fantail; Break-o'day Boy for the Pied Butcherbird; Poor Soldier for the Noisy Friarbird; and Chocolatebird for the Speckled Warbler.

Myna or Miner?

The Noisy Miner is a honeyeater.

*W*ithin the honeyeater group there are four species that share the name of miner (previously mynah). These species are the Bell, Noisy, Yellow-throated and Black-eared Miners. All of these species are robust birds with yellow-coloured bills and legs. They are predominantly tree-dwellers that search for insects, honeydew and berries on the leaves, branches and bark, but they may also visit the ground. Miners are native to Australia.

Enter a New Myna

Another bird was introduced into Australia in the mid- to late nineteenth century. This bird also has a yellow bill, legs and feet. It is, however, a myna, and a member of the starling family. The Common Myna lives happily among humans and has established itself in large numbers in almost every urban area along Australia's eastern and southeastern coasts.

Although the miners and mynas are quite dissimilar in both appearance and habits, the similarity in their names has created much confusion in distinguishing between them. This has arisen predominantly from the name, which has often lead people, mistakenly, to place the birds in the same group, as well as fuelling many household arguments as to which spelling applies to which birds.

The introduced Common Myna is a member of the starling family.

A Brown Treecreeper: note its specialised claws for climbing.

Brown Treecreeper   16–18cm

Of the seven treecreepers found in the world, six are found in Australia (the seventh is found in New Guinea). The Brown Treecreeper, a common and familiar bird, lives in the drier open forests and woodlands of eastern Australia. Its call, a loud 'spink', uttered either singly or in a series, generally betrays its presence before the bird is observed.

The Brown Treecreeper has predominantly pale brown plumage. The head, throat and upper breast are pale greyish brown, while the lower breast and belly are strongly streaked with black and buff. The eyebrow is more buff than that of the White-browed Treecreeper and a buff wingbar reveals itself when in flight.

As with other treecreepers, food is obtained by clinging to the trunks and branches of trees and probing into cavities with the long downwardly curving bill. The Brown Treecreeper also feeds on the ground, where it consumes largely ants but other insects and their larvae are also taken.

Grey Shrike-thrushes usually pair for life.

Grey Shrike-thrush   22.5–25cm

Ranging throughout Australia, the Grey Shrike-thrush is a common and familiar bird. Its alternate names of Harmonious Shrike-thrush and Whistling Shrike-thrush have stemmed from its beautiful whistling song, which echoes loudly throughout the variety of wooded areas that it inhabits. Typically songs include phrases such as 'pip-pip-pip—pip-hoee' and a sharp 'yorrick' but phrases unique to individual birds are often uttered, too.

The song somehow makes up for the bird's rather drab plumage, which varies throughout its extensive range. While mostly grey in the east, with an olive-grey back and pale grey-white cheeks and underparts, in the north the plumage is predominantly brown and western birds are grey with buff underparts. The Grey Shrike-thrush has a varied diet, including insects, spiders, small mammals, frogs, lizards, birds' eggs and young birds.

Grey Shrike-thrush pairs generally remain together for life and inhabit the same areas throughout this time, maintaining breeding territories of up to 10 hectares. Both birds build the nest and share incubation duties and care of the three or four young birds that are born each year.

Black-faced Monarch 16–19cm

This beautiful bird, with a blue-grey head, throat and upperparts, a black face and russet underparts, is perhaps the most familiar of the monarchs. It is an inhabitant of rainforests and wet sclerophyll forests, where its presence is announced by its distinctive 'why-you-which-yew' call. Only the male sings and during the breeding season he sings incessantly, even when sitting on the nest. Apparently constructed solely by the female, the nest is an

Male Black-faced Monarchs sing on the nest.

elaborate woven cup of fine stems, often casuarina needles and spider webs, decorated externally with green moss.

The Black-faced Monarch belongs to one of two distinct groups of monarchs within Australia, its distribution stretching along the east coast as far as Melbourne. Within its group and sharing similar colouring is the rare Black-winged Monarch, which is only found in the northern Cape York region as a summer breeding migrant from New Guinea, and the Spectacled Monarch, another east coast species but only to the New South Wales–Victoria border.

Rufous Fantail 15–18cm

Within Australia, there are five species of fantail. Of these the Rufous Fantail is undoubtedly the most colourful. Its range extends in a broad coastal band from the Kimberley, Western Australia, through northern and eastern Australia to western Victoria. The Rufous Fantail prefers the wetter forest and woodlands, and is a familiar sight in rainforests, dense eucalypt forests and mangroves.

Similar in habits to other fantails, it actively forages among the foliage for insects. Its long grey-brown tail, with bright rufous base, is fanned out as

The Rufous Fantail is an active insect hunter.

it busily flits from tree to tree. The rump is also rufous in colour, as is the forehead, while the remaining plumage is brown above and white below, with black mottling on the throat. The Rufous Fantail is a confiding and inquisitive bird, and often approaches close to an observer. It is a strongly migratory species, especially in the southern part of its range, and is more common in the north.

Why don't I Find Dead Birds in the Bush?

*T*he length of a bird's natural life varies according to its habits, diet, habitat and natural or introduced threats. Generally, smaller songbirds have the least chance of surviving to become breeding adults, whereas seabirds have the greatest. Studies have shown that of all the eggs laid by small songbirds, only approximately 10 per cent will survive to breed. Of this 10 per cent, about 70 per cent will die within the first year. In seabird species, however, only 3 per cent are expected to die each year.

Only 10 per cent of small songbirds reach breeding age.

So where do all the thousands of songbirds that must die each year go? Predation by other birds, mammals and reptiles certainly accounts for the majority of bird deaths. The remainder that die from disease or fall out of the nest, are quickly cleaned up by the natural recyclers of the bush, such as ants, decomposing organisms and scavengers that readily feed on carrion.

How Long do Birds Live?

*I*t is almost impossible to reliably measure the age of wild birds without some system of identification that can distinguish the bird, such as unusual plumage coloration or tagging. In cases where these identification markers have been used, studies have shown that seabirds have the highest longevity records.

The record for the longest lived species is for a Royal Albatross that had lived to 58 and was still breeding. There are indications that albatrosses may live for over 100 years but this has yet to be proved. As a rule, larger birds are expected to live longer than smaller ones. Birds that are held in captivity generally live to a greater age than those in the wild. Perhaps the most reliable record for a captive bird's age was that of a Sulphur-crested Cockatoo that was living at London Zoo in 1982. This particular bird had been given to the zoo in 1925 and before that it had been in the care of a person since 1902.

The Sulphur-crested Cockatoo is one of the longest lived birds.

How Many Young do Birds Have?

Some birds lay large numbers of eggs in a year so as to increase their chances of producing offspring that will attain breeding status. Other species, such as many of the albatrosses, lay only a single egg, and breed only once every two years. If this single egg or chick does not survive, it can seriously affect the long-term viability of that species' population.

Many Baskets or One Big Mound

Other birds, such as parasitic cuckoos, lay several eggs,

The Shining Flycatcher lays 2–3 eggs in a clutch.

each in a different nest. Putting all your eggs in one basket is a practice observed by 'mound-building' species, such as the Orange-footed Scrubfowl, the Australian Brush-turkey and the Malleefowl. These birds construct enormous mounds of leaf litter and other vegetation in which to incubate their eggs. The eggs are buried deep inside the mound and the heat generated by rotting vegetable matter is used to incubate them. The birds carefully regulate the heat by adding and removing quantities of leaf litter. Some mounds are wholly constructed and maintained by a single male. In such cases, if something happens to the male carer, many offspring are lost. In other mound-builders, a single mound may be constructed and utilised by several pairs.

The incubation mound of Malleefowl may contain up to 33 eggs.

RECORD EGG-LAYERS

The European or Common Cuckoo has been recorded as laying up to 25 eggs in a single season. Other species, such as the Cowbird, have been documented as laying more than 30 eggs in a single season and the mound-building Mallee Fowl of Australia may incubate up to 33 eggs in a single mound.

Magpie-lark

26–30cm

Although the Magpie-lark is a mud-nest builder, it is unrelated to Australia's other mud-nesting species.

Also called the Peewee, the Magpie-lark is confined to Australasia. The alternative name has arisen from its harsh 'pee-o-wit' or 'pee-wee' call. During the breeding season birds often sit side by side calling as they raise and lower their wings. Magpie-larks have bold black and white plumage. Males have black foreheads and throats and distinct white eyebrows; females have all-white faces, and young birds have white throats, black foreheads and white eyebrows.

The Magpie-lark is found throughout Australia in all but the densest forests and driest deserts. In Tasmania it is a rare vagrant and it is also found in Timor and New Guinea. It is largely terrestrial and is most often seen slowly searching the ground for a variety of insects and their larvae, earthworms and freshwater invertebrates.

Dressed For Combat

The Magpie-lark is an aggressive defender of its nest and territory, which may occupy up to 10 hectares. Both sexes select the nest site and construct the nest, which is made from mud procured from nearby pools. Both, too, share incubation duties and care of the three to five young. If conditions are favourable more than one brood may be reared in a year. Non-breeding and young birds form large flocks, often consisting of several thousands of individuals; they move nomadically in response to changing weather patterns. It is easily distinguished from the much larger Australian Magpie by its size.

> **MUD NESTS**
>
> The Magpie-lark, Apostlebird and White-winged Chough all have the unusual habit of building nests almost entirely of wet mud; these are shaped into bowls and allowed to dry. Similarities in nesting habits have often led to the three species being grouped together, but DNA tests show that the Magpie-lark is related to the flycatchers, while the other two belong to another family.

The Australian Magpie feeds on insects and their larvae.

Australian Magpie 36–44cm

This large black and white bird is found in all but the densest forests and most arid deserts throughout Australia. It is a common and familiar bird, especially on open grassy areas with scattered trees, where it walks along the ground in search of insects and their larvae, which form the bulk of the bird's diet.

Its conspicuous plumage varies throughout its range. The nape, upper tail and shoulders are white in all forms and in most cases the remainder of the body is black. but birds from Tasmania and the southeast, centre and extreme southwest of the mainland have an entirely white back. In addition to this, the white of the upperparts are more grey in the female birds.

Groups of up to 24 birds live year round in territories that are actively defended by all members of the group. The group depends on this territory for all their feeding, roosting and nesting requirements. The Australian Magpie's loud musical flute-like song has earned it the uncommon alternative name of the Flute Bird.

A Pied Currawong: note the yellow eye.

Pied Currawong 44–51cm

This large black and white bird is often confused with the Australian Magpie but the Pied Currawong is almost entirely black with large patches of white in the wings and a white base and tip to the tail. Unlike the Australian Magpie, the bill is wholly black and the eye is yellow.

There are two other species of currawong in Australia. The Grey Currawong lives throughout the south, while the Black Currawong is restricted to Tasmania. Both species differ from the Pied Currawong in having no white on the rump.

The Pied Currawong is found in forests and woodlands throughout eastern Australia and is a common bird around suburban areas. The name 'currawong' was derived from the 'currawong' call of the Pied Currawong. Other calls include guttural croaks and a wolf whistle. Currawongs feed on a variety of foods including small lizards, insects and berries, and their penchant for young birds has made them an unpopular species among bird lovers.

Bowerbirds

*A*ustralia is home to 10 of the 19 species of bowerbirds found in the world: eight live only in Australia, the other two occur in New Guinea as well. Two of the Australian bowerbirds are called cat-birds due to their wailing cat-like calls. The nine species absent from Australia are exclusive to New Guinea. Historically there has been much debate about the relation-ship between bowerbirds and the birds of paradise but recent studies have shown that bowerbirds are most closely related to crows and butcherbirds.

A Fawn-breasted Bowerbird. Inset: a Great Bowerbird displaying his crest.

Courting in the Bower

Bowerbirds are so named because of their unique courtship behaviour that takes place in con-structions called 'bowers'. These bowers are built by the males and are decorated with a variety of natural and artificial articles. The bowers are designed to seduce female birds that are attracted by the males' advertis-ing calls. Once in the area of the bower, a male leaps into a series of spectacular displays that are further intended to persuade the female into allowing him to mate with her. Once mated, the female will fly off to construct a nest and raise the young, in most cases unassisted by the male. In this way the male will attempt to mate with as many females as possible.

Bowerbirds feed predominantly on fruits, especially figs, and some flowers, leaves and insects. Young birds are fed almost entirely on insects. Catbirds frequently kill the nestlings of other bird species to feed to their own young.

COLOUR DIFFERENCES

In most cases, male bowerbirds that inhabit the wetter forests tend to be brightly coloured, whereas those from the more arid areas are relatively drab. These drab birds do, however, have a brightly coloured patch on the nape, which is normally only visible during display.

Great Bowerbird   32 to 37cm

Found across northern Australia, this dull, fawn-coloured bird with darker mottled upperparts inhabits the rainforest fringes, drier eucalypt forests and riverine woodlands. Its striking lilac crest situated on the rear of the neck is revealed only during courtship displays and is much reduced or absent in females.

The male constructs a large bower, with two parallel, interwoven stick walls. These are decorated with a variety of objects, including bones and shells. Females are attracted to the bower by a series of calls, including mimicry of other bird species and machinery. Once a female is attract-

The female Great Bowerbird is drab in comparison to the lilac-crested male.

ed, the male attempts to seduce her with a series of exaggerated and contorted displays. As with most other bowerbird species, the mated female performs all nesting duties, while the polygamous male breeds with many females. The Great Bowerbird is a wary bird and its drab plumage makes it difficult to observe amongst the foliage but its undulating flight is characteristic.

Paradise Riflebird   25 to 30cm

Of the four birds of paradise found in Australia, three are riflebirds. Each are somewhat similar in plumage, the males being glossed black, subtly tinged with iridescent purple and blue-green, while the females are predominantly brown. The Paradise Riflebird is the only bird of paradise found south of the Tropic of Capricorn: as far south as Barrington Tops, New South Wales. The Magnificent Riflebird lives in far northern Queensland, while the Victoria's Riflebird is found at the base of Cape York Peninsula, Queensland.

The Paradise Riflebird is a bird of paradise.

As with the other two species, the Paradise Riflebird has a short square tail and long, downwardly curved bill. As it skilfully walks up the trunks of trees it probes this bill into crevices in search of insects and their larvae. It also takes berries and fruits. The courtship display is spectacular and is characteristic to all riflebirds. The male selects a perch in the sunlight and arches his wings above his head. He then tilts his head back and moves it in a mechanical fashion to highlight the metallic colours of his throat.

Where Have All My Blue Pegs Gone?

Male Satin Bowerbirds collect blue objects for decoration.

*P*erhaps the most well known bowerbird, particularly along the eastern coast of Australia where it is found, is the Satin Bowerbird. Bowerbirds are renowned for pilfering things from humans to decorate their bowers and the male Satin Bowerbird has a penchant for bright blue and violet coloured objects. This preference may or may not be linked to his glossy blue-black plumage and violet-blue irises.

Commonly among his assortment of parrots' feathers, flowers and berries are such human paraphernalia as blue pegs, bottle tops and straws. Bowerbirds have been known to pilfer jewellery, cutlery, coins and one bower was even found to have a glass eye.

Are all Bowers the Same?

*T*here are four types of bowers. Each varies in size, shape and intricacy. The simplest is the 'stage' type used by the Tooth-billed Bowerbird. This consists of a cleared area of forest floor decorated with leaves. The 'mat' type bower is used by Archbold's Bowerbird found in New Guinea. It consists of a bed of dried fern stems decorated with snail shells and the bodies of beetles and berries.

The most commonly constructed bower is the 'avenue' type. This consists of two vertical parallel walls of interwoven sticks and grass stems with a cleared display area at each end.

The fourth type is an elaborate construction called the 'maypole' type bower. The Golden Bowerbird is the only Australian species to construct it. Two small trees about a metre apart, with a fallen branch in between provide the foundation. The male piles twigs up the sides of both uprights, forming two columns which after successive uses may reach three metres in height.

A Golden Bowerbird, architect of the maypole bower.

What is the Trumpet Bird?

*M*ore commonly known as the Trumpet Manucode, the Trumpet Bird is a bird of paradise species that favours the established tropical rainforests of northern Cape York Peninsula, south to the Iron and McIlwraith Ranges. Both sexes are black, with a greenish blue gloss, and both have a bright red eye.

Trumpet Manucodes differ from other Australian birds of paradise in that males are monogamous, that is they only mate with one female and both share the raising and care of the young.

Although the Trumpet Manucode superficially resembles the Spangled Drongo and the Metallic Starling in its colouring, any confusion is instantly dispelled when its booming, trumpet-like call is heard. The unique sound is made by the male, which has a long, coiled trachea, overlying the muscles of the breast. This sound gave the bird its common names of Trumpet Manucode or Trumpet Bird.

The striking Trumpet Manucode is more often heard than it is seen.

Bird Mythology

*B*irds of paradise were so named because the first specimens to reach Europe were not live birds but skins sent as gifts from the Molluccas to the King of Spain. The Molluccans called the birds *Bolon diuata*, meaning birds of God.

The skins were used by the Molluccans for ceremonial purposes. During their preparation the legs and wings were removed. This gave rise to a long held myth that these birds were legless, never coming to Earth and that the female laid her eggs in a hollow on the male's back while in perpetual flight.

When birds of paradise such as this were first discovered, it was believed they never landed.

Grassfinches

Both the Zebra Finch (above) and the Beautiful Firetail (right) are Australian grassfinches. Grassfinches are popular aviary birds.

Of the approximately 124 species of grassfinch known throughout the world, 20 live in Australia. Only the Nutmeg Mannikin and the Black-headed Mannikin are introduced. The Nutmeg Mannikin is a native of Southeast Asia and was introduced into Australia in about 1930, while the Black-headed Mannikin is native to India and was introduced in the early 1920s. While the Black-headed Mannikin has not been reliably recorded since 1981 and is now believed to be extinct, the Nutmeg Mannikin has flourished.

The native grassfinches exhibit remarkable plumage variation, which has lead to their widespread popularity as cage-birds. Perhaps most striking is the Gouldian Finch, resplendent in its bright yellow, purple and green plumage, with a red, black or yellow face mask.

Grassfinches feed mostly on grass seeds and supplement this diet with insects. They are also monogamous and most are believed to keep the same partner for life.

SMALL BUT NUMEROUS

By far the most numerous grassfinch is the Zebra Finch. These small, predominantly grey birds, with white underparts, chestnut-coloured cheeks and barred black and white tails, form huge flocks of thousands of individuals in the arid grasslands of Australia.

The Humble Relations

Only recently has it been discovered that sparrows and grassfinches are closely related and they now fall within the same family. Both the House Sparrow and Eurasian Tree Sparrow were introduced into Australia in the 1860s. The House Sparrow has successfully spread throughout eastern Australia and is common wherever there is human habitation. The Eurasian Tree Sparrow is confined to the southeast.

The Red-browed Finch feeds in flocks.

Red-browed Finch 10–12cm

This finch can be distinguished by its bright red rump and red eyebrow. The remainder of the body is olive-green above and grey below. The Red-browed Finch is distributed in a broad band along the east coast of Australia and a small population of escaped aviary birds exists near Perth, Western Australia. Found in open forests, grasslands, agricultural areas and urban parks and gardens, these birds are seldom far from water, their high-pitched 'seeee' or 'ssitt' call accompanying their every movement.

The Red-browed Finch forms quite large flocks that feed on a variety of ripe and half-ripe grass seeds, supplemented with fruits, herbs and some insects. The flocks are quite confident around humans and are often easy to observe at close range. Both parents build the bulky, flask-shaped nest, normally placed a few metres off the ground within a spiky bush. Both parents care for the five to eight young and non-breeding birds have often been observed helping rear chicks from other broods.

The striking Long-tailed Finch from northern Australia needs to drink regularly.

Long-tailed Finch 13–16cm

This striking grassfinch can be identified by its fawn brown upperparts, pinkish brown underparts, blue-grey head and nape and black throat. The tail is black and thread-like, with a contrasting white base. Across its range, which extends from the north of Western Australia to northwestern Queensland, its bill colour changes from yellow in the west to orange-red in the east. Young birds have black bills throughout.

The Long-tailed Finch inhabits dense grasslands with scattered trees close to water, feeding on grass seeds and insects. The Black-throated Finch of eastern Australia is strikingly similar in both plumage and habits, but it lacks the long tail and has a black bill. Both species are usually seen in small flocks of 20 to 30, but larger flocks may congregate in the drier areas. Breeding takes part in loose colonies. The female constructs the nest while the male gathers the nesting material.

Where did Australian Birds Come From?

*M*any of Australia's bird species are found only in Australia, others belong to groups that are found only within the Pacific region; the remainder are part of more international families. This diversity has fuelled much discussion about the origins of Australia's birds. Research into this area is still in its infancy but of all the hypotheses that have been put forward about where our birds came from, one stands out as far more convincing than all the rest.

Emus are uniquely Australian, but similar birds such as Africa's Ostrich suggest that both are derived from a common ancestor.

The Gondwanan Connection

About 100 million years ago Australia was part of a super-continent called Gondwana. At this time Australia was between one and two thousand kilometres south of its current position. On this super-continent many birds roamed freely and, when it divided into the separate continents, many birds became isolated. For the stronger fliers, it was still possible to travel between the new continents but other species were stranded. As Australia moved closer to Asia, many bird species from these two continents became able to fly between the two regions. So, it appears that some of Australia's birds are the result of those left stranded on the continent when it broke up and others are derived from Asian birds.

Cassowaries roamed freely in Australia and New Guinea when the two lands were joined.

Land Bridges

This theory is further reinforced by the resemblance of numerous Australian species to those of other continents that separated from Gondwana; for example, Australian Emus and African Ostriches. The movement of species was still going on as recently as the last ice age, approximately 10 000 years ago. At this time, there was a land bridge that extended from New Guinea to Australia. This land bridge allowed many species to move from the drier areas of lowland Australia to the wetter, upland areas of northern Australia and on into New Guinea.

Human Introductions

There are, however, many other factors that have since contributed to the composition of the present-day populations. The movement of birds around the world has also been influenced by humans, who have introduced many species to 'foreign' lands. These introductions have been both intentional and accidental but all have had a serious negative impact on the country's native species.

The Spotted Turtle-Dove was introduced into Australia.

Why Were Some Birds Introduced?

*O*ver the years many species of birds, as well as other animals and plants, have been introduced by humans into many different areas of the world. These introductions have been both deliberate and accidental. Captive birds were transported for the purposes of food and navigation and they often escaped or were released.

In the nineteenth and early twentieth centuries organisations named Acclimatisation Societies introduced hundreds of species into many countries around the world. The birds were liberated for many reasons, including food, sport, controlling pests or the simple fact that the birds were nice to look at, had a pretty song or just reminded the settlers of their homeland.

While some species have had little impact on their new environment, most have had an undesirable effect on the native species. Once established, the introduced birds compete for food and breeding sites, and have forced a reduction in native bird numbers and also their distribution.

Since its introduction in 1862, the Common Blackbird has established itself in Australia's southeast.

AUSTRALIA'S OLDEST BIRD

Australia's oldest bird record dates back some 125 million years. The bird was approximately the size of a Grey Shrike-thrush but it was distinctly different from our modern-day species. The group to which this bird belonged became extinct around the same time as did the dinosaurs.

Introduced Birds

The introduced House Sparrow and Laughing Turtle-Dove (inset).

Over the years, many species of birds have been introduced into Australia. Most of these have become well established, particularly around urban areas, but some have not succeeded.

Most of the introduced birds are common and familiar around gardens. The Spotted Turtle-Dove was introduced from southern Asia in about 1870 and is now a common sight in most urban gardens. Similarly, the Laughing Turtle-Dove, found in Western Australia, was introduced from Africa and southern Asia. The House Sparrow, Eurasian Tree Sparrow and Common Starling have followed European settlers, and the Common Myna has become well established since its introduction from Southeast Asia during the 1860s.

A High Level of Establishment

Other introduced birds include the Red Junglefowl, Ostrich, Common Pheasant, Indian Peafowl, Wild Turkey, California Quail, Mute Swan, Rock Dove, Skylark, Red Bishop, White-winged Widowbird, Nutmeg Mannikin, Black-headed Mannikin, Common Chaffinch, European Greenfinch, European Goldfinch, Common Redpoll, Red-whiskered Bulbul, Common Blackbird and Song Thrush. Most of these species are found within eastern Australia following their introductions in major capitals along that coast. All but the Red Bishop, White-winged Widowbird and Black-headed Mannikin are now well established.

> **LAND DIVINING**
> The earliest reliable record of people deliberately introducing birds is from before 800 AD, when Norse voyagers released caged birds from their ships to ascertain their proximity to land. If the birds did not return to the ship, the seamen assumed land was near.

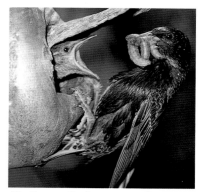

The Common Starling is a major fruit pest.

Common Starling   20–22cm

The Common Starling was introduced into Australia in the late 1850s. It originated from Europe where it was once a common bird of the deciduous woodlands but it now favours more urban areas. In Australia it has also become a familiar sight around human habitation throughout the east and southeast.
It is also a prominent bird in open cultivated areas and is a well-known pest of orchards, although it feeds on insects and their larvae as well.

The Common Starling shows considerable variation in plumage. Both adults resemble each other, although the female is considered less glossy than the male. In autumn, the plumage is glossed black with a purple and green iridescence. The feathers have buff tips, which gives the bird a spotted appearance. These spots are almost completely absent from birds in spring. During the breeding season, August to January, the bill and legs are yellow, becoming brown at other times. Young birds are grey-brown, becoming a glossier black with age.

Red-whiskered Bulbuls sing sweetly.

Red-whiskered Bulbul   20–22cm

The Red-whiskered Bulbul is a native of southern Asia. Since its introduction into Australia in 1880, it has become a familiar sight in Sydney's urban parks and gardens where it feeds on a variety of native and introduced fruits, supplemented with insects. Birds were also successfully introduced into Melbourne but no records are available as to when this occurred.

Although, the Melbourne population has remained fairly concentrated, from Sydney the Red-whiskered Bulbul has spread to many areas along the east coast. It is instantly identifiable by its pointed black crest. The remaining plumage is brown above, with a white cheek and throat, mottled underparts and a reddish undertail. The red whisker from which it derives its name is situated below the eye but is often difficult to see. It is a confident bird around humans and will often allow a close approach as it calls sweetly from a telegraph pole or the high perch of a bush.

PIGEONS & PARROTS

Are Pigeons and Doves the Same?

*T*he pigeons and doves are a widespread family of stout-bodied and short-legged birds, with over 300 species found throughout the world. In most instances they are medium-sized birds with small-sized heads and short to medium length tails.

Some species, such as the Victoria Crowned Pigeon and the other goura pigeons, reach quite large sizes and are decorated with elaborate plumes. While quite a few species are rather drab, others, such as Australia's Wompoo Fruit-Dove, are beautifully coloured with greens, purples, yellows and greys.

The group feeds predominantly on fruits and seeds, and in most the call is a soft cooing. Scientifically, there is no distinction between pigeons and doves. In most cases the word dove, which is Anglo Saxon in origin, is applied to the smaller species, while pigeon, which is a French word from the Latin *Pipionis* meaning a young chirping bird, is applied to the larger species. This is not a steadfast rule however.

The Crested Pigeon is widespread.

How Do Homing Pigeons Find Their Way?

*H*oming or racing pigeons are descendants of the Rock Dove. They have long been used for relaying messages, even as far back as the early Egyptians. Although this practice died out with the introduction of telegraphy and radio, it found a useful resurgence during the both world wars. The pigeons were released by airmen that crashed at sea and by the German Resistance. In total there were over a quarter of a million birds used, although the success was fairly limited due to the highly mobile nature of many of the camps.

Homing pigeons use a variety of influences to find their way.

Pigeons are able to navigate their way using a variety of influences, such as the stars, the sun, visual landmarks, internal programming and the Earth's magnetic field, but in what proportion we have yet to measure. Certainly, some individuals are more successful 'homers' than others; whether this is an indication that some methods used for navigating are better than others is uncertain.

Are Australia's Pigeons Safe from Extinction?

*A*lthough the pigeons and doves of Australia's interior are relatively common and secure, the tree-dwelling species associated with the eastern coast are considerably less common. These species are largely frugivorous, that is they feed on a variety of fruits.

Trees fruit at different times in different areas and so the birds must travel, often quite long distances, between suitable feeding grounds. The clearance of habitat and the associated absence of continuous tracks of suitable vegetation, or wildlife corridors, have posed a major threat to the survival of many species. Many of them have been forced to withdraw from much of their range but, at present, none have become extinct.

Wompoo Fruit-Doves are vulnerable to habitat clearance.

Sudden Population Collapses

Even though the numbers of many of the arid area pigeons may seem secure at present, we should not be complacent. The famous Passenger Pigeon of North America was found in numbers of hundreds of millions. Reports of the skies being darkened for several hours by a single flock were not uncommon. Due to factors such as habitat clearance, shooting and a mysterious disease, the Passenger Pigeon was virtually wiped out within a single year. The last known bird, a female called Martha, died in Cincinnati Zoo in 1914.

The ability to suck up water is a pigeon speciality.

DRINKING HABITS
Unlike many other birds that sip water, pigeons are able to drink large quantities at one go. The bill is submerged in the water and the bird drinks by sucking. The only other Australian birds that are able to drink in this way are some of the grassfinches.

The Rock Dove is common around cities.

Rock Dove 33–36cm

The Rock Dove, also known as the Feral or Street Pigeon, is found in close association with human settlement throughout much of the world. This association dates back to when they were domesticated by the Egyptians over 6000 years ago.

While there is no real indication as to when the species was introduced into Australia, large numbers of birds have been documented since the early to mid-nineteenth century. Although found in huge numbers in most major centres, they have not ventured far from human settlement. Although primarily seed-eaters, Rock Doves will also investigate and eat most scraps and, on any street, birds can be seen pecking at the ground in a never-ending search for food.

It is native to Europe, Africa and Asia, where it prefers open agricultural areas. The Rock Dove breeds along coastal cliff faces, as well as artificial cliff faces, such as apartment buildings with accessible ledges or roof spaces.

Native Bar-shouldered Doves drink regularly.

Bar-shouldered Dove 27–31cm

The Bar-shouldered Dove is a native to Australia. It inhabits the wetter forests and woodlands, and vegetation along creeks and rivers. It ranges across northern and eastern Australia but has declined in numbers since the introduction of the Spotted Turtle-Dove.

Its slender build, brown upperparts, with distinct black edging to each feather, russet nape, grey face and throat and pale underparts should easily identify it. It is most often encountered singly or in small groups, usually feeding on seeding grasses and herbs. When disturbed, it normally flies swiftly to a nearby tree, the flight lacking the undulating pattern of other doves of similar size.

The Bar-shouldered Dove is fairly sedentary. Most individuals stay in a particular area throughout the year but some have been recorded ranging quite widely, presumably if food or water become insufficient. These doves are never found far from water as they need to drink regularly. Their common call is a triple 'coo' or 'kook-a-wook'.

Crested Pigeons have a whistling flight.

Crested Pigeon   30–35cm

This native pigeon is common in much of mainland Australia. Found in any habitat with the exception of the denser forests and wetter coastal areas, it is seldom far from water.

There are only two Australian pigeon species that possess a crest. The Spinifex Pigeon is markedly smaller, with cinnamon-coloured plumage and a bright red facial patch. The Crested Pigeon is a robust, soft pink and grey pigeon, with a long black crest and a small pinkish red ring around each eye. If startled it takes to the air with a characteristic whistling flight and glides with downturned wings; upon landing, it swings its tail high in the air. The whistling sound is produced by the air passing a pair of reduced primary wing feathers.

The Crested Pigeon is often encountered alone or in small parties busily feeding on the ground or perching on a sunlit tree branch. Food consists mostly of seeds, although some leaves and insects are taken.

Common Bronzewings have iridescent wings.

Common Bronzewing   30–36cm

The Common Bronzewing is found in all but the most arid areas and densest rainforests, and is one of the most abundant of Australia's pigeons. When observed it is normally in small parties, feeding on the ground on seeds. It is a very wary pigeon and seldom allows close approach. If startled it flies strongly and directly. Rarely far from water, small groups gather to drink at waterholes during the day or night.

The Common Bronzewing can be identified by its pinkish grey breast and paler brown back, with iridescent patches of green, blue and red in the wing. It has a conspicuous white line below and around each eye. The male has a yellow-white forehead and a darker pink breast.

The related Brush Bronzewing, which is found in southern Australia, is smaller and its head and shoulders are a more chestnut colour. Both species emit the deep 'oom' call, normally repeated several times; although it is slightly higher in pitch in the Brush Bronzewing.

Can Birds Talk?

Certain species, such as the parrots and mynas, are able to mimic the patterns of human speech. Other birds can mimic human words and sounds but their vocalisations do not follow the same vowel patterns; they merely copy the pitch. Why only some birds are able to copy human vowel patterns is a mystery.

Although evidence suggests that wild birds do not 'talk', there have been instances where bushwalkers have heard a Sulphur-crested Cockatoo say a human word or phrase. Whether these birds have escaped from captivity or have adopted a vocabulary due to a close association with humans is uncertain.

Captive Galahs are wonderful mimics of human speech.

Talking Incentives
In captivity, birds develop the powers of speech best when they are kept away from other members of their own kind. The birds become intimate with their keeper and learn to obtain more attention by talking. This explains why the birds talk more when you are not paying them attention than when you are showing their abilities off to another person.

What Colour Should a Budgie Be?

The Budgerigar is native to Australia. Since its discovery by John Gould in 1794 it has become internationally popular as a cage-bird. The first captive breeding was initiated in about 1840 by John Gould's cousin, Charles Coxon. Since then it has been bred into a variety of colour forms, including pure white, blue, yellow, mauve, olive and grey. Naturally, the

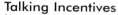

Wild budgies are green and yellow, with black barring above and a small blue patch on the cheek.

> **ROASTED BUDGIE**
> The Australian Aborigines had several names for the Budgerigar. The current name is derived from one of these, 'Budgery-gah'. The first part of this name translates as 'good', while the second part means 'food' or 'to eat'. The young chicks are taken from the nest and quickly roasted before eating.

Budgerigar is green and yellow, with black barring above and a small patch of blue on its cheek. Yellow birds are an uncommon naturally occurring colour form called lutino. White or albino birds are also naturally found.

Where Have All the Parrots Gone?

*A*ustralia is blessed with over one-sixth of the world's parrot species. Unfortunately, about one-third of these are endangered. There are three main contributing factors to this decline.

Widespread habitat clearance is the first activity which is threatening many parrot species. Parrots require hollows in mature trees for nesting. Many of the trees containing appropriate hollows are felled to make land available for agriculture or are destroyed by fire.

White-tailed Black Cockatoos are popular overseas as cage-birds.

The lack of suitable hollows is evidenced by reports of birds sharing hollows for nesting or occupying a hollow as soon as the young from another pair have left the nest. Even in protected areas, the trees are damaged by bush-fire and hollows are destroyed by poachers as they extract the eggs or young birds.

Further Population Pressures

Illegal trapping has become a more serious threat since parrots have had to contend with habitat loss. Parrots are relatively long-lived species and can sustain a few breeding seasons where the young are lost but if they are not breeding successfully to start with, the loss of young to poachers is more significant.

The introduction of feral predators, such as cats, foxes and dingoes, has also had an effect on parrots. Ground-nesting species, such as the Night Parrot, have been eliminated from much of their previous range due to widespread habitat loss. In the areas that remain suitable for them they are now threatened by these feral predators. Tree-dwelling species are also under threat from the feral cat, which is a skilled climber. People can help parrots thrive by leaving old hollow trees standing, even if dead.

Major Mitchell's Cockatoos command a high price on the black market.

Parrots

A pair of Gang-gang Cockatoos feeding on winter berries.
Inset: A Musk Lorikeet reaches for eucalypt blossoms.

The parrot group consists of both parrots and cockatoos. Within Australia there are 14 species of cockatoo and 38 species of parrot. A further three parrot species were known to occur in Australia but have now been declared extinct.

Species such as the Galah, Little Corella, Red-tailed Black-Cockatoo, Budgerigar and Varied Lorikeet can be found in enormous, noisy flocks of several hundreds, often several thousands, while others, such as the Glossy Black-Cockatoo are quite rare. The Paradise Parrot, is unfortunately famed for being the first mainland Australian bird species to be declared extinct, while the Night Parrot has not been positively sighted for over 50 years. A dried body of the Night Parrot was found recently in southwestern Queensland however, which has revived the search for conclusive evidence of its continued existence.

> **SMALLEST PARROT**
> With a body length of only 13 cm, Australia's smallest parrot is the Double-eyed Fig-Parrot. This species feeds on native fig seeds along the eastern coast of Australia from northern New South Wales to Cape York Peninsula in Queensland.

The Origin of Parrots

Of Australia's 52 species, 43 are found nowhere else in the world and the three extinct species were also unique to Australia. Although the origins of the parrot group is still very much in debate, the fact that the majority of the world's 332 species are found in South America and Australia, as well as Africa, India, New Guinea and New Zealand, suggests that they originated in Gondwana, the supercontinent that existed 100 million years ago and contained each of these countries.

Cockatiels are widespread inland.

Cockatiel   30–33cm

The Cockatiel, or Quarrion as it is popularly called, is actually a cockatoo, although its slender body and long pointed tail is more characteristic of a parrot. It is wide-spread throughout mainland Australia but large numbers are found in the more arid inland areas, where it can be seen feeding on a variety of grass seeds, nuts, berries and grain. Feeding may take place either on the ground or in trees.

The Cockatiel's predominantly grey plumage with white wing patches, orange cheeks and a distinctive crest make it unmistakable. The male differs from the female by having a bright yellow forehead, face and crest. Although mostly silent, the Cockatiel utters a prolonged and distinctive 'queel-queel' in flight. A popular cage-bird, second only to the Budgerigar, the Cockatiel is an affectionate pet. Free-flying flocks, however, have a characteristic beauty that adds to the uniqueness of the Australian outback.

A Crimson Rosella in adult plumage.

Crimson Rosella   32–36cm

Although the adult Crimson Rosella is distinctive in its rich crimson plumage with bright blue cheeks, young birds have caused much confusion. Most young birds have the characteristic blue cheeks but the remainder of the plumage is a mixture of greens, reds and blues. The young bird gradually attains the adult plumage over a period of 15 months. In adult birds the back and wings are black, with each feather broadly edged with red, and the wings have a broad blue patch along the edge.

The Crimson Rosella is commonly associated with the tall eucalypt and wet-ter forests of southeastern Australia and its harsh, ringing 'cussik-cussik' is a familiar sound in these areas. Sometimes, when perched, it makes a soft 'pipping' sound. Two distinct populations of this species exist in Australia. The northern Queensland population is smaller and darker.

Crimson Rosellas are normally encountered in small flocks and are readily attracted to garden seed trays; once familiar, they will readily accept hand-held food.

77

OTHER BIRDS

Can Birds Make it Rain?

While birds cannot make it rain, there are several Australian species that have been associated with inclement weather. Their colloquial names arose as a result of their sudden appearance at the onset of a bad rainy spell or at the commencement of the rainy season in Australia's north.

A number of birds are known locally as Rainbirds, including the Pallid Cuckoo, Common Koel, Channel-billed Cuckoo and the Grey Currawong. The Pallid Cuckoo

The raucous Channel-billed Cuckoo.

and Common Koel are also known sometimes as the Stormbirds, as are White-throated Needletails, and Oriental Pratincoles are referred to as Little Storm-birds.

Bird Barometers

The Pallid Cuckoo is found throughout Australia and is a regular migrant to the country's north. Although its breeding is confined to the period from August to January in the south, it may breed at any time in the north, providing suitable conditions are available. Its loud, monotonous call, which it uses to advertise for a mate, heralds the start of the rainy season.

The Common Koel and the largest of the parasitic cuckoos, the Channel-billed Cuckoo, are also regular migrants to Australia's north and east. Their arrival each year coincides with the onset of the north's rainy season.

White-throated Needletails are a wide-ranging species. Their movements are linked with changes in atmospheric conditions and they arrive in Australia with the warm, humid air that travels ahead of thunderstorms and carries an abundance of insects. These birds may sometimes be seen congregating around bush-fires where insects are plentiful.

Grey Currawongs are found throughout southern Australia.

RAINBIRD OF THE SOUTH

The Grey Currawong is resident to southern Australia and remains in the same area for most of the year. It is thought that it acquired is name of Rainbird from its ringing call, a familiar sound in areas subject to high amounts of drizzling rain.

Which Bird Calls All Night Long?

*I*n September each year the Common Koel arrives from India and New Guinea. Light sleepers are immediately aware of its presence — it has a habit of calling 'ko-el, ko-el, ko-el' incessantly during the night. The call, repeated in a rising pitch, is also made during the day.

The Common Koel, 39–46 cm in length, is a member of the cuckoo family. The male's glossy black plumage is tinged with blue and green and he has a striking red eye. The female and young birds are more cryptically coloured with glossed brown upperparts, heavily spotted with white, and a black crown. The underparts are more buff with numerous fine black bars.

Male Koels account for many sleepless nights.

Koels parasitise the nests of larger honeyeaters, such as wattlebirds, friarbirds and the Blue-faced Honeyeater, as well as figbirds and the Magpie-lark.

Which Cuckoos Build their own Nests?

*T*he coucals are a widespread group of large, ground-dwelling cuckoos that do not rely on the help of other birds to raise their young. Coucals are found in Australia, Africa, New Guinea, the Philippines and New Britain. The single Australian representative is the Pheasant Coucal. Coucals construct nests in low bushy trees or on a flattened grass tussock. A loose, untidy construction of grass stems and fine sticks, lined with leaves, these nests may be sphere-shaped if elevated off the ground or bowl-shaped and surrounded by grasses pulled over to act as a cover if in a

The Pheasant Coucal lives mostly on the ground.

tussock. The two to five swollen white eggs are incubated for up to 15 days, with the emerging young taking a further 10 to 15 days to leave the nest.

Cuckoos

A Horsfield Bronze-Cuckoo. Inset: Black-eared Cuckoo.

*I*n Australia there are 13 species of cuckoo, which represent 10 per cent of the world's cuckoos. Some of these are migratory and only arrive in Australia at certain times of the year. Two species, the Oriental Cuckoo and Chestnut-breasted Cuckoo, are not known to breed here. All but the Pheasant Coucal are parasitic, laying their eggs in the nests of other birds.

The parasitic cuckoos have a specific range of species that they use as foster parents or hosts for their young. Of the ten breeding parasitic cuckoos found in Australia, there have been more than 200 recorded hosts. The female lays a single egg in the nests of several host birds and eliminates one of the eggs already in the nest. As she is able to closely match the appearance of the host's eggs, the host normally accepts the new cuckoo egg as one of its own.

DECEITFUL EGGS

If a cuckoo's egg does not closely match the size, colour and pattern of those already laid by its host, it is usually laid in an enclosed nest where the light is poor. These are normally dark, highly patterned eggs, that are difficult to distinguish in the restricted light.

Bye Bye Baby

In most cases, once the young has hatched, it ejects the other eggs and hatchlings from the nest by manoeuvring them to the perimeter of the nest and then, using the flattened area in the middle of its back, forcing them up the side and over the edge. In other species the cuckoo's egg is able to hatch quicker than the other eggs and so the young cuckoo out-competes the other smaller hatchlings for food.

A fledgling Pallid Cuckoo being fed.

Pallid Cuckoo 28–33cm

This large cuckoo is almost hawk-like in appearance. In open wooded country throughout Australia it is the most common and widely distributed of cuckoos. It is instantly identified by its grey plumage and broadly barred black and white undertail. No other Australian cuckoo has this coloration. Younger birds are more brown and buff on the back and wings.

The Pallid Cuckoo lays its eggs in other birds' nests, including those of flycatchers, honeyeaters, woodswallows, whistlers, the Willie Wagtail and the Hooded Robin. Its call

is a loud, ascending 'too-too-too...' that is often repeated incessantly and has given rise to the name of Brainfever-bird. As with most other cuckoos, its call normally indicates its presence long before it is seen. The Pallid Cuckoo particularly likes hairy caterpillars but takes other insects and larvae.

Fan-tailed Cuckoos have an upright stance.

Fan-tailed Cuckoo 24.5–28.5cm

Throughout eastern Australia and south-western Western Australia and Tasmania the descending mournful trill of the Fan-tailed Cuckoo is familiar, particularly during the breeding season, which is between August and December in the east and June to October in the west.

Host species include flycatchers, fairy-wrens, scrubwrens and thornbills, particularly the Brown Thornbill. The Fan-tailed Cuckoo inhabits open wooded areas, where it is often seen perching on a low, exposed branch. When sighted, it can be identified by its dark grey upperparts and soft buff underparts. The black tail is notched with white above and barred black and white below. On landing, the tail is often raised before the bird assumes its more characteristic perching stance. It can be distinguished from the superficially similar Brush Cuckoo by its bright yellow eyering.

Like the Pallid Cuckoo, the Fan-tailed Cuckoo enjoys hairy caterpillars but it will also take a variety of other insects and their larvae. Outside of the breeding season, birds are generally nomadic; those in Tasmania migrate to the mainland at this time.

Owls

*A*ustralian owls are divided into two groups. The masked owls, which have a heart-shaped facial disc, and the hawk owls, which have an indistinct facial disc. Of the ten owl species that have been recorded in Australia, they are evenly divided, with five belonging to each group. One of the hawk owls, however, the Brown Hawk-Owl, has only been recorded as a rare vagrant.

Masked Owls

The five masked owls are the Sooty, Lesser Sooty, Barn, Masked and Grass Owls. The latter three are somewhat similar in plumage. The upperparts are brown, ranging from sandy orange in the Barn and Grass Owls to blackish brown in the Masked Owl. Each have paler underparts and conspicuous spotting. The Masked Owl is the largest at 35 to 50 cm, while the other two are 30 to 39 cm in length. The Sooty and Lesser Sooty Owls are dusky grey. Both are confined to the eastern coast, with the Lesser Sooty Owl found only in the north of Queensland.

Above: A Barn Owl. Right: a Southern Boobook.

SHARP SENSES
An owl's ear openings are quite large. They are able to detect the movements of their prey and capture it, even in complete darkness. The eyes are also well suited to hunting. They are situated at the front of the bird's head, which gives a narrower and more acute field of vision, called binocular vision.

Hawk Owls

The hawk owls include the Barking, Rufous, Powerful Owls and the Southern Boobook. All are mottled brown in plumage with large yellowish eyes. The Barking Owl, 35–45 cm, is found in wooded areas throughout much of Australia, where its rapid, barking 'wook-wook' call is characteristic. The Rufous Owl, 46–57 cm, is confined to Australia's north, where it is uncommon. The large Powerful Owl, 56–60 cm, is found in the tall eucalypt forests of the southeast. It, too, is uncommon. The Southern Boobook, 25–35 cm, is by far the most common of all of Australia's owls, being found in a variety of habitats throughout Australia.

A Tawny Frogmouth mimicking a branch.

Frogmouths

Owls are not the only nocturnal birds within Australia. There are also frogmouths, nightjars and an owlet-nightjar. Of these the frogmouths are the largest. The Tawny Frogmouth, 34–53 cm, shows great variation in size throughout its large range, which covers the whole of Australia. Birds are larger in the southeast than in the north and can be identified by generally silvery grey plumage, streaked and mottled with black and rufous; they have large yellow eyes. Some birds are more russet red than grey.

The Papuan Frogmouth, 50–60 cm, is found only in the woodlands and rainforest fringes of Cape York Peninsula, Queensland, and has orange-red eyes. The Marbled Frogmouth, 36–45 cm, with mottled brown plumage and orange-yellow eyes, is confined to the rainforests of central eastern Australia and far north Queensland. The Tawny Frogmouth is found only in Australia, while the other two species are also found in New Guinea and the Solomon Islands.

The small Australian Owlet-nightjar.

Nightjars and Owlet-nightjars

There are three nightjars in Australia. The Spotted Nightjar, 29–31 cm, is by far the most common. It is found in open woodlands and neighbouring plains in all but the extreme east and southeast. In flight, two large white spots are visible at its wingtips. Other plumage is predominantly grey-brown with numerous buff spots; it is the only nightjar with an all-white throat. The Large-tailed Nightjar, 27–29 cm, also has white spots on its wings but can be distinguished by its white outer tail feathers. This species is found along the fringes of wet forests in the far north and northeast. The White-throated Nightjar, 32–37 cm, inhabits wooded areas along the eastern coast of Australia. The plumage is much darker than the others and the white throat is divided in two by a distinct, broad black line. When in flight it can be distinguished by the absence of white markings on the wings or tail. The small Australian Owlet-nightjar, 21–25 cm, is common throughout Australia. It is generally russet brown to grey, with faint black barring.

Does That Branch Have Eyes?

*W*hen you are out walking in the forests or woodlands you may get the feeling that something is watching you. The mere branches of the trees and pieces of fallen wood seem to grow eyes. It is not a scene from *The Wizard of Oz*; what you are seeing are frogmouths and nightjars.

By day these nocturnal insect-feeders cleverly camouflage them-

A roosting White-throated Nightjar is well camouflaged and easily overlooked.

selves in the trees or leaf-litter. Their cryptically coloured brown and grey plumage, with numerous spots and streaks, allow them to blend in with their surroundings. Here they sit motionless until dusk, only moving slightly if disturbed. The frogmouths camouflage themselves as tree branches, while the nightjars turn to pieces of wood or bark on the ground.

> **FLASHY EYES**
> Nocturnal birds can be seen at night, using a torch or spotlight. When the light is flashed on them, their eyes reflect a red coloration. The Australian Owlet-nightjar is the only nocturnal species whose eyes are non-reflective to lights.

How Can Owls Fly So Quietly?

A feather is a complex structure made from dead cells that have been filled with a substance called keratin. The keratin contains an enzyme that is resistant to attack and so they can last quite a long time. Flight feathers have a central shaft and a vane on either side of this. The vanes are made of single filaments that have barbs protruding from them. It is these barbs and the smaller barbules, attached to each barb, that interlock each filament giving the feather its rigid structure and preventing the separation of one feather from another during flight.

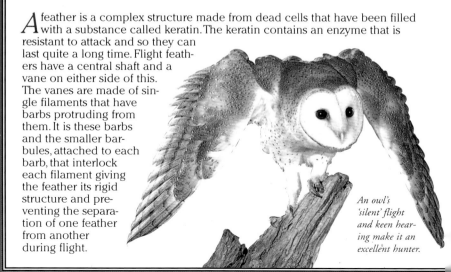

An owl's 'silent' flight and keen hearing make it an excellent hunter.

In owls, the barbules are unusually long and reduce the amount of rubbing of each over-lapping feather. This adaptation, in addition to long, curved barbs on the leading edge of each flight feather that reduce air turbulence, allow the owl to adopt the silent flight that it uses to sneak up on its prey. The remaining body feathers are also softer than in many other species of bird. These help to muffle any sound the bird makes as it flies through the night.

> **SPINNING HEADS**
> Owls are misleadingly thought to be able to twist their heads in a complete 360 degree circle. While they do have great mobility in this area, the actual rotation is only up to about 270 degrees.

Do Bee-eaters Only Eat Bees?

*R*elated to the kingfishers, bee-eaters are conspicuous, brightly coloured birds that sit patiently on an exposed perch. When an insect flies past, the bird will actively pursue it, returning to the perch to consume its meal. All bee-eaters do eat bees and other venomous insects such as wasps and hornets. They are able to expertly de-sting their prey, by rubbing and bashing the insect against a perch, before eating it.

In certain species, honeybees make up almost their entire diet, although in other species the percentage of bees taken can be quite low. Typical other insect prey includes dragon-flies, flies, grasshoppers and beetles. Certain bee-eater species have been recorded as eating small lizards, although this is highly unusual, bee-eaters preferring flying prey as a rule. Even a perched insect is totally ignored until it takes flight. Once it is airborne, however, the bee-eater springs into action. In the same way as kingfishers, bee-eaters consume their prey whole (with the exception of the sting) and the indigestible bits are regurgitated later in pellets.

The only bee-eater found in Australia is the Rainbow Bee-eater. This slender bird measures 21 to 28 cm in length, including its elongated tail shafts (when present). It is unmistakable with its beautiful blue-green body, rufous crown and conspicuous black line through the eye. In flight the wings are bright rufous-orange below. The call, a high-pitched 'trrrrp-trrrrp', is given mainly in flight.

The Rainbow Bee-eater is found in a variety of habitats, with exception of denser forests, throughout the Australian mainland.

The Rainbow Bee-eater is very appropriately named, both for its colour and its diet.

Kingfishers

*T*he ten kingfishers found in Australia belong to a large family that comprises some 90 species throughout the world. The bee-eaters and rollers are also closely related. The Australian kingfishers vary quite markedly in size, plumage and habits. The largest are the kookaburras, the Laughing Kookaburra measuring some 45 cm and the slightly smaller Blue-winged Kookaburra about 40 cm. The smallest is the aptly named Little Kingfisher at just 12 cm.

A Collared Kingfisher. Inset: a Sacred Kingfisher inspects a possible nesting spot.

The Australian kingfishers can be split into two groups. The first includes both the river or water kingfishers and the second, the forest kingfishers.

River Kingfishers

Both the Azure and Little Kingfishers feed on small fish, insects and crustaceans. They are both found in well-vegetated riverine areas, swamps and mangroves. The Azure Kingfisher, 17–19 cm, is widely distributed throughout northern and eastern mainland Australia and Tasmania, whereas the Little Kingfisher is confined to Australia's north and northeast.

Forest Kingfishers

The forest kingfishers feed mainly on land animals, although the Collared Kingfisher, 23–29 cm, and the closely related Sacred Kingfisher, 19–23 cm, also feed on crustaceans and small fish. The little studied Yellow-billed Kingfisher, 18–21 cm, inhabits the dense rainforest and mangrove areas of Australia's extreme north but is also found in offshore islands and New Guinea. The migrant Buff-breasted Paradise-Kingfisher, 29–36 cm (including its magnificent long tail), is perhaps the most striking of all the kingfishers. It arrives in the rainforests of northeastern Queensland in spring each year and returns to New Guinea after breeding.

Kookaburras are large kingfishers.

Laughing Kookaburra   40–45cm

The raucous, chuckling 'koo-koo-koo-koo-koo-kaa-kaa-kaa' 'laughter' of this familiar bird is a feature of the Australian bush. The Laughing Kookaburra, or Laughing Jackass, is found throughout eastern Australia and the extreme southwest of Western Australia. Here it inhabits most areas where there are suitable trees. In the central north and northwest of Australia it is replaced by the slightly smaller Blue-winged Kookaburra. The two do overlap in central and eastern Queensland, although the Blue-winged Kookaburra tends to occupy more coastal areas.

The Laughing Kookaburra can be distinguished by generally white underparts, faintly barred with dark brown, a brown back and brown wings with a contrasting blue patch. The tail is rufous and broadly barred with black rather than blue, as in the Blue-winged Kookaburra, and it has a broad dark brown eye-stripe.

The Laughing Kookaburra also has a shorter 'koooaa', which is normally given when accompanied by other birds. The call of the Blue-winged Kookaburra is coarser and ends somewhat abruptly.

Dollarbirds are seasonal breeding migrants.

Dollarbird   26–31cm

The Dollarbird is a migrant to Australia, arriving in September each year to breed. The name is derived from a large blue-white spot on each wing, resembling American dollar coins in size and shape. The remaining plumage is dark brown, glossed with blue-green on the back and wings. The bill is orange-red, finely tipped with black.

The Dollarbird is the sole Australian representative of the roller family, so named because of their rolling courtship display flight. In northern and eastern Australia, it inhabits open wooded areas, normally with mature, hollow-bearing trees. It requires hollows for nesting and the three to four white eggs are cared for by both parents. The young birds are fed on flying insects.

Although the breeding season ends in about January each year, the Dollarbird remains in Australia until about April before returning to New Guinea, the Solomons and the Philippines. The distinctive, harsh 'kak-kak-kak' call is repeated several times and is often given in flight.

How are Swiftlets Different from Swifts?

A White-throated Needletail roosting.

There are some 85 species of swifts and swiftlets found throughout the world. Six of these are found in Australia. Both swifts and swiftlets have wide mouths, designed for scooping up insect prey, and their sleek bodies, with long tapered wings, are highly manoeuvrable and well-suited to their aerial existence.

Swiftlets are smaller and more slight than the swifts. Three of the species found in Australia — the Glossy and Uniform Swiftlets and the House Swift — occur only as rare vagrants. The remaining species are the White-rumped Swiftlet, a breeding resident of northeastern Australia, the Fork-tailed Swift and the White-throated Needletail. The latter two species are non-breeding migrants, arriving in Australia each October and departing for their Asian breeding grounds in about April or May, sometimes August if conditions are favourable.

Do Swifts Ever Land?

The White-rumped Swiftlet is known to roost in caves but two swifts were, for many years, thought never to land at all during their time in Australia. All activities, including sleeping, were believed to happen in the air. This misconception was firmly held until the mid-1970s when several roost sites were discovered. Radio-tracking has now confirmed that these swifts roost in tree hollows, normally returning to the same site each night. Having forward-facing toes with sharp claws, swifts are well-suited to clinging to vertical surfaces.

RECORD FLIERS

While the White-throated Needletail has been recorded achieving a speed of up to 130 km per hour, the fastest recorded flying speed for a bird is attributed to the Peregrine Falcon, which, when in a dive, may reach in excess of 180 km per hour.

Stooping at speeds exceeding 180 km per hour, the powerful Peregrine Falcon is the world's fastest bird.

What's in Birds' Nest Soup?

*S*wifts and swiftlets develop large salivary glands when breeding. The swiftlets use this saliva, in conjunction with other materials such as cobwebs, moss and other plant material, to construct their nests. The swiftlet creates a semi-circle of saliva on the proposed nest surface, which dries quickly and forms the foundation of the nest.

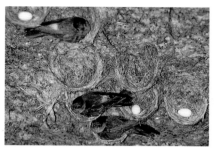

White-rumped Swiftlets nest in colonies.

The Edible-nest Swiftlet of Southeast Asia constructs a nest entirely of saliva. The quick-drying saliva is applied in layers until the cup- shaped nest is complete. These nests are highly-prized, being harvested for the famed birds' nest soup, a delicacy of Chinese cuisine. The nests are harvested at the completion of the breeding season, with numbers exceeding 300 000 from a single cave in Rongkop, central Java. The nests are also prized as an aphrodisiac and may be served as a jelly, either spicy or sweet.

Is it a Swift or a Swallow?

*B*oth swifts and swallows have long pointed wings, short, weak legs and wide beaks designed for catching insects. They both follow a largely aerial existence and it is this lifestyle that has led to their similarities. They are, in fact, from two different families. Swifts share a family with the swiftlets, while swallows are grouped with the martins.

FINDING HOME IN THE DARK

Certain species of swiftlet use echo-location to navigate within the total darkness of caves. By emitting a series of clicks and examining the returning echoes they are able to determine the position of solid objects, such as their nests.

Unlike swifts, which are usually airborne, this Welcome Swallow, like all swallows, will often land.

Do Birds Pair For Life?

Yellow-nosed Albatrosses pair for life. Only if one bird dies will the other search for a new mate.

*I*n most species, breeding birds form monogamous relationships. That is they pair with a single partner. The majority of monogamous birds pair with a different partner each season but some, such as many species of grassfinches and albatrosses, stay with the same partner for life. In these species, pairs usually keep close social bonds throughout the year.

Males of certain species, such as many of the bowerbirds, birds of paradise and emus, have more than one mate or are polygamous.

Multiple partners are not only restricted to males. The females of certain species may have several males in tow. These relationships are termed polyandrous.

A pair of Budgerigars reinforcing their lifelong bond.

Who Looks After The Young?

*A*fter breaking through the shell of their egg, many chicks are completely dependent on their parents until they are able to leave the nest, in some cases up to nine months later. Others, such as the chicks of mound-building birds like the Australian Brush-turkey, must fend for themselves from the moment they hatch. There are many species that fall in the middle of these two extremes. The parental roles also vary between species.

In the majority of the bowerbirds, the female is required to construct the nest, incubate the eggs and care for the young on her own. The female emus and jacanas have it quite the reverse. Once the eggs are laid, the male is in sole charge. In species such as the European Goldfinch, the female performs all the incubation duties, being fed at the nest by the male, but both feed the young hatchlings.

In most cases, however, both parents share both the incubation duties and feeding of the young.

The male Emu is in sole charge of the eggs and chicks.

What Sort of Binoculars Should I Buy?

*B*inoculars are the most important piece of birdwatching equipment. Do not rush out and purchase a pair with the most powerful magnification; they are not necessarily the best and you may be wasting your time and money.

All binoculars are stamped, usually close to the eyepiece, with the magnification and diameter of the object glass; for example 7 x 40 or 10 x 50. The most important thing is to choose a pair that offers good light-gathering potential. This can be easily assessed by dividing the second number by the first; the number obtained, known as the exit pupil diameter, should be at least five. To find out what brands are good, talk to other birdwatchers and ask them what they recommend.

Binoculars are the most important piece of birdwatching equipment and can be the most expensive.

When viewing a bird through your binoculars, try to position yourself so that the sun is behind you. You will see the bird's colouring better this way. With the sun behind the bird, all you will see is its silhouette.

A Checklist of Australian Bird Families

The following is a list of all the families of Australian birds:

Emus & Cassowaries
(Family Casuaridae)

Mound-builders
(Family Megapodiidae)

Quails
(Family Phasianidae)

Magpie goose
(Family Anseranatidae)

Ducks, Swans & Geese
(Family Anatidae)

Grebes
(Family Podicipedidae)

Penguins
(Family Spheniscidae)

Petrels & Shearwaters
(Family Procellariidae)

Albatrosses
(Family Diomedeidae)

Storm-petrels
(Family Hydrobatidae)

Tropicbirds
(Family Phaethontidae)

Gannets & Boobies
(Family Sulidae)

Darters
(Family Anhingidae)

Cormorants
(Family Phalacrocoracidae)

Pelicans
(Family Pelecanidae)

Frigatebirds
(Family Fregatidae)

Herons
(Family Ardeidae)

Ibis & Spoonbills
(Family Threskiornithidae)

Storks
(Family Ciconiidae)

Hawks & Eagles
(Family Accipitridae)

Falcons
(Family Falconidae)

Cranes
(Family Gruidae)

Crakes & Rails
(Family Rallidae)

Bustards
(Family Otididae)

Button-quails
(Family Turnicidae)

Plains-wanderer
(Family Pedionomidae)

Curlews & Sandpipers
(Family Scolopacidae)

Painted Snipe
(Family Rostratulidae)

Jacanas
(Family Jacanidae)

Sheathbills
(Family Chionidae)

Stone-curlews
(Family Burhinidae)

Oystercatchers
(Family Haematopodidae)

Stilts & Avocets
(Family Recurvirostridae)

Plovers & Dotterels
(Family Charadriidae)

Pratincoles
(Family Glareolidae)

Gulls & Terns
(Family Laridae)

Pigeons & Doves
(Family Columbidae)

Cockatoos
(Family Cacatuidae)

Parrots & Lorikeets
(Family Psittacidae)

Cuckoos
(Family Cuculidae)

Coucals
(Family Centropodidae)

Hawk Owls
(Family Strigidae)

Masked Owls
(Family Tytonidae)

Frogmouths
(Family Podargidae)

Nightjars
(Family Caprimulgidae)

Owlet-nightjars
(Family Aegothelidae)

Swifts & Swiftlets
(Family Apodidae)

River Kingfishers
(Family Alcedinidae)

Forest Kingfishers
(Family Halcyonidae)

Bee-eaters
(Family Meropidae)

Rollers
(Family Coraciidae)

Pittas
(Family Pittidae)

Lyrebirds
(Family Menuridae)

Scrub-birds
(Family Atrichornithidae)

Treecreepers
(Family Climacteridae)

Australian Wrens
(Family Maluridae)

Pardalotes, Scrubwrens,
Gerygones & Thornbills
(Family Pardalotidae)

Honeyeaters & Chats
(Family Meliphagidae)

Robins & Flycatchers
(Family Petroicidae)

Logrunners
(Family Orthonychidae)

Australian Babblers
(Family Pomatostomidae)

Whipbirds & Quail-thrushes
(Family Cinclosomatidae)

Sittellas
(Family Neosittidae)

Whistlers & Shrike-thrushes
(Family Pachycephalidae)

Monarch Flycatchers
(Family Dicruridae)

Cuckoo-shrikes
(Family Campephagidae)

Orioles & Figbirds
(Family Oriolidae)

Woodswallows &
Butcherbirds
(Family Artamidae)

Birds of Paradise
(Family Paradisaeidae)

Ravens & Crows
(Family Corvidae)

Mud-nesters
(Family Corcoracidae)

Bowerbirds
(Family
Ptilonorhynchidae)

Larks
(Family Alaudidae)

Pipits & Wagtails
(Family Motacillidae)

Sparrows & Grassfinches
(Family Passeridae)

Sunbirds
(Family Nectariniidae)

Flowerpeckers
(Family Dicaeidae)

Swallows & Martins
(Family Hirundinidae)

Grass Warblers
(Family Sylviidae)

White-eyes
(Family Zosteropidae)

Thrushes
(Family Muscicapidae)

Starlings
(Family Sturnidae)

INDEX